Research Reports Esprit

Project 8749 · ORCHESTRA · Volume 1

Edited in cooperation with the European Commission, DGIII/F

Esprit, the Information Technology R&D Programme, was set up in 1984 as a co-operative research programme involving European IT companies, IT "user" organisations, large and small, and academic institutions. Managed by DGIII/F of the European Commission, its aim is to contribute to the development of a competitive industrial base in an area of crucial importance for the entire European economy. The current phase of the IT-programme comprises the following eight domains: software technologies, technologies for components and subsystems, multimedia systems, long-term research, open microprocessor systems initiative, high-performance computing and networking, technologies for business processes, and integration in manufacturing.
The series *Research Reports Esprit* is helping to disseminate the many results – products and services, tools and methods, and international standards – arising from the hundreds of projects that have already been launched, involving thousands of researchers.

Springer
Berlin
Heidelberg
New York
Barcelona
Budapest
Hong Kong
London
Milan
Paris
Santa Clara
Singapore
Tokyo

Nuno Guimarães (Ed.)

Organizational Change, Evolution, Structuring and Awareness

Organizational Computing Systems

Springer

Volume Editor

Nuno Guimarães
INESC
R. Alves Redol 9
P-1000 Lisboa, Portugal

Cataloging-in-Publication Data applied for

Die Deutsche Bibliothek - CIP-Einheitsaufnahme

Organizational change, evolution, structuring and awareness :
organizational computing systems / Nuno Guimarães (ed.). - Berlin ; Heidelberg ; New York : Springer, 1998
(Research reports ESPRIT : Project 8749, ORCHESTRA ; Vol. 1)

CR Subject Classification (1991): H.4.1–3, H.5.3

ISBN-13:978-3-540-62863-7 e-ISBN-13:978-3-642-80399-4
DOI:10.1007/978-3-642-80399-4

Publication No. EUR 18173 EN of the
European Commission, Dissemination of Scientific and Technical Knowledge Unit,
Directorate-General Telecommunications, Information Market and Exploitation of Research,
Luxembourg.

Typesetting: Camera-ready by the editors
SPIN: 10486606 45/3142-543210 – Printed on acid-free paper

Preface

The Orchestra (Organizational Change, Evolution, Structuring and Awareness) project, as the name suggests, was the result of the contributions of a number of people and organizations, whose collaborative efforts made the project and its results possible. This report provides readers with a global perspective on the project, its conceptual roots, the developed technologies, the partners, and the users.

The following subsection is a long but necessary acknowledgement to a large number of people, from the several organizations that participated in the project: INESC (P), SMD (P), Software AG (D/E), UPM (E), Lisle (E), Novabase (P), EDP (P), Edinfor (P), CN (P), ISCTE (P), UITESA(E), TASKON (N). Without these organizations and the people mentioned below, the project would not have been possible. The uninvolved reader is therefore asked to forgive us for this long acknowledgement, and go directly to the first chapter.

Acknowledgments

This is a personal acknowledgment of the contributions of most of those people, and an anticipated apology to anyone who may have been left out of this large list. The persons are mentioned in the order of the organizations they belong to, just for the sake of not losing track of them all.

From INESC, thanks to João Gonçalves for his permanent awareness of the administrative and financial procedures and status of the project; to Armando Vieira for the help in the management of the technical documentation and periodic reporting of the project; a very special thanks to Ana Paula Pereira for her continuous support and availability to perform the difficult task of bridging heterogeneous teams involved in the organizational diagnosis, as well for her help in preparing final scenarios and documents, and intermediating between several partners; to Pedro Antunes for his work on the negotiation and decision tools, along with Tânia Ho and Isabel Soares who saw themselves involved in a larger task than they had asked for; to Luís Carriço for his comments and observations in the diagnosis area; to Adriano Couto for his excellent technical work and his role as interface between INESC and SMD; to André Zuquete who did much more than his job on the security system and helped to set up much of the computer platforms for demonstrations and integration (besides having a restored heart in between); to Paulo Guedes for his interest and push in INESC and at SMD; to Nuno Duarte, Gonçalo Nunes, and Cândido Manso, for their conclusive work in the communications tasks; to Lúcia Costa and Cláudia Mesquita for their enthusiasm and availability in taking the responsibility of coordinating the marketing and exploitation analysis; to João Barreira for supporting that effort; to José Alves Marques for the decisive push during the negotiation phases of the project; and to Paula Monteiro and Madalena Azevedo who helped in so many administrative tasks that the project required, and to to Pedro Quintela for helping in several demonstrations.

At SMD, I have to thank Mário Romão for his permanent availability, even at times when other commitments probably deserved higher priority, as well as for his understanding of the social protocols involved in the project; to José Luís Mota for his acute sense of participation and support, before the approval of the project and afterwards, in several reviews and meetings; to Helena Oliveira, Marco Paulo, José Bernardo Silva, and Fernando Faria, who directly or indirectly designed, developed, and lived with the project's decisions.

From Novabase, thanks to Filipe Carlos for the quality of his work in the Workflow system, to José Fernando Sousa for the contributions in the definition of a synergistic agreement between SMD and Novabase, together with Pedro Carvalho and to Filipe Monteiro for his participation in the initial meetings when the proposal was configured.

At Edinfor, a special thanks to Carlos Raposo, who never missed a request or a meeting and managed the relation with EDP particularly well; to Paula Simões and Pedro Coelho for the support in the networking setup between INESC and Edinfor; to Ricardo Rahal who made a difference in spite of a late contact with the project; to Pinto da Fonseca, António Rua, Venceslau Parreira, Luís Delgado and Fernando Vidigal, for their collaboration and participation in several of the tasks concerning EDP, Edinfor, and Software AG; and, last but not least, to António Vidigal for his interest in the project and his support.

In EDP, a first word for Leuschner Fernandes, for his constant concern for all the details of the participation of EDP in Orchestra. João Amaral and Isabel Carapinha deserve a special word for their concerned participation in a project that got in the way of their daily responsibilities at Sines.

At CN, I must thank Francisco Silva for his constant interest that went beyond the limited universe of CN and that stimulated long and rich conversation, to Fernando

Nunes for his professional execution of the work and constant support in the installation of the pilot, to the staff that helped in the demonstration at the project's review that took place in CN, and to the president of CN, Eurico Cabral da Fonseca, for his support and interest in the project.

In UITESA, Carmen Izquierdo and Cristina Rubio have done their best to build a useful and interesting pilot at CONUC. Diego Molina, head of CONUC was always present and interested, and provided all the possible support to the project, to the head of UITESA, for his support before and after the project's approval.

In Software AG, José António Frias has been the best possible coordinator, always available and willing to contribute to the progress of the project. Fernando García Julián, Fernando Centeno, and Pedro Basagoiti carried out their technical tasks with responsibility and competence, together with Irma Trueba, María Carmen Barrera, Pablo Ribes, and Ricardo Alvaro. José Ignacio Milan, the head of Software AG in Spain and beyond, has been decisive in supporting the participation of Software AG, including in the intermediation with Peter Schnell, Hoerst Kinzinger, and Bernd Jerschensky, in Germany, who also showed their interest in the project. António Alagoa, head of Software AG in Lisbon provided all the help we needed with technology and particular configurations and installations. Luís Reis, and António Rodrigues also made their contribution during the negotiation phase, and afterwards when SAG's technology was deployed.

Odd Arild Lehne, from Taskon, was a perfect partner, always interested, available, and ready to make high quality contributions to the technical and managerial actions of the project. Anne Hurlen left the project very soon because of a happy event, a baby, but gave her support in the initial phases. Gro Oftedal, Gunnar Bo, Thomas Grimeland, Per Helge Carlsen and Jorn Andersen did their best in the integration of Taskon/OORAM with other components of the project.

At UPM, Jesús Cardeñosa was an enthusiastic participant of Orchestra. Javier Segovia gave us a valuable push in the tasks shared with INESC, together with Daniel Borrajo, in the beginning of the project. Christèle Legeard managed all the administrative issues with diplomacy. The technical team composed of Julio García del Real, José Antonio Espinosa, Victor Gímenez, Lourdes Moreno, Carlos Juárez, Angel Morales, Guillermo Pastor, Gilles Reyna, Javier Carbó, Germán Cancio, and Caridad Anías, did a very fine job in the tasks of contextual communication and the decision and negotiation system.

In ISCTE, Luís Reto was an inspiring partner. Carlos Pé-curto, Teresa Veloso and Paula Santos did their best in the diagnosis processes. Francisco Nunes and Albino Lopes were always ready for discussion and valuable contributions. Correia Jesuíno and Gomes Cardoso gave their best support to the setup and execution of the project.

In Lisle, a word for Carlos Brazão for his energy in the initial phases of the project, and the contributions to the definition of the Orchestra marketing approach; thanks to Rafael Lopez for his readiness in the dramatic occurrence of the Madrid meeting, when a transceiver was desperately missing; and to Piedad Arias for her early contributions.

Finally, a special word to three persons who "played" along in the Orchestra project. Ralph Hansen, as Commission Project Officer, helped us in managing a large and often complex project. Peter Lau and Margaret Gardiner, as reviewers of the project, have always been supportive and expressed a positive view of the project, helping us to tune our work and results. The outcome of the project would not be the same without them, and became much better through their contribution.

Lisbon, August 1997 Nuno Guimarães

Table of Contents

1. Introduction

This document constitutes the final report of the Orchestra (Organizational Change, Evolution, Structuring and Awareness) project, Esprit 8794. This report is addressed to the European Industry and IT community, and aims at providing a comprehensive perspective on the project's goals, activities, experience and results. This perspective is presented from both the technical, research and development, and marketing point of views.

This report is also meant to be an inspiring description of a project in the broad area of Organizational Computing, useful to industrialists, managers, developers and researchers in the area. In this context, it provides a global perspective of the challenges that underpinned the project definition, a brief history of the creation of the project and some critical analysis of achievements, benefits, difficulties and adjustments that have progressively been identified and encountered during the project. This perspective and analysis is justified by the fact that, while projects have limited time spans, limited objectives, and limited resources, they cannot be seen as an isolated set of activities and efforts. From our perspective, Orchestra will have impact in several industrial, development and research directions in the next few years. In summary, this report is an open-ended document, hopefully interesting to readers external to the project.

The organization of the report is the following:

- The overall project presentation identifies the rationale behind the project, the industrial, sociotechnical and research objectives. It includes a short description of the genesis of the project and the steps that led to the design and production of the proposal.
- The technical definition of the Orchestra results is an environment, made up of technical and integrated components, as well as principles and methodologies. The role of the methodologies and the functionality of the several components is presented in chapter 3.
- The Orchestra architecture, depicting the several modules and their integration principles and techniques, is presented next. A relevant aspect in this architecture is the set of API (Application Programming Interfaces) provided by the system, which assure its extensibility and tailorability in the future.

- Chapter 5 provides additional technical details or overview technical specifications of each one of the Orchestra components. This chapter can be skipped in an initial reading of this report and revisited for a more detailed information on particular components (like platforms, hardware & software, implementation languages, etc.).
- The role, activities and lessons learned from the work at the pilot sites is outlined in chapter 6. Here, we intend to stress the contribution of each pilot site, but also to draw lessons from the approach that was taken in their integration with the technical tasks of the project.
- Chapter 7 refers marketing and exploitation. As such, it is a summary of a deeper analysis and planning that is included in the companion reports (Market Analysis, Product and Service Definition, and Exploitation Plans).
- Chapter 8 presents the role and contribution of the partners in order to provide an understanding of the mutual interactions that occurred in the execution of the project.
- The dissemination of results achieved in some industrial and research *fora* is presented in chapter 10.
- A final chapter, entitled conclusions outlines the most significant achievements of the project, from our own perspective, and proposes evolutions of these achievements based on the present state-of-the-art, in both the industrial and research domains, on the needs that have been perceived in the period of preparation and execution of the project, Fall 1992 to Fall 1996, and on the lessons learned.
- The references essentially include documents produced in the project and other literature that backs up decisions taken in the project or assumptions made in this final report.

The document tries not to assume the knowledge of previous documents, namely the project's Technical Annex or any of the three previous Progress Reports. Moreover, it refers whenever adequate, to the deliverables that have been produced by the several partners during the execution of the project.

The Appendices include a number of additional information. The list of deliverables is presented in the Appendix A. The documents themselves are packaged in the Orchestra CD-ROM that aggregates the project's documents and additional information[1]. Appendix B lists the organizations and concrete persons that are able to provide the readers with additional information on the particular aspects of the project. Appendix C presents the result of an internal survey that addressed the expectations and conclusions of the several people involved in the project.

---

[1] Further information concerning the availability of this CD-ROM can be requested to the editor, Nuno Guimarães, nmg@inesç.pt | guimaraesn@acm.org

2. Rationale and Birth of the Orchestra Project

This chapter presents the Orchestra project. An outline of the reasoning framework that underlies the project's objectives and configuration is presented first. The objectives are then identified and a summary of the history of the project is included.

The presentation of the conceptual framework of Orchestra is included to provide an understanding of how the project has been created from a set of ideas and a global, high level approach, to the relation between organizational theory and information technology. This framework tries to relate both domains without arguing for the uniqueness of the organizational perspective used for this reasoning.

The objectives of project are a more concrete explanation of what we were trying to achieve in technological terms. However, the socio-technical issues are also mentioned and the set of attributes that we envisaged for the technological results of Orchestra are not completely orthogonal to the organizational views.

The historical record of the design and production of the proposal, including administrative data, is meant to enlighten readers on the process of building such a project, in terms of time and effort. It is a particular view of the project manager, enriched, whenever possible, with impressions from other members of the Orchestra.

2.1 A Conceptual Framework

Organizational computing systems are aggregates of computer-based artifacts and tools that support, influence and provide cohesion to the activities performed by groups of people engaged in achieving common goals.

From the technology viewpoint, organizational computing systems benefit from the advances in interactive and distributed systems, increased connectivity and increased information and activity sharing among users. From the social side, and just as Human Computer Interaction is highly influenced by psychology and cognitive sciences, organizational computing systems absorb models and concepts from social sciences in general, and organizational studies in particular. The rationale for this project can be summarized as follows:

> *A systematic and acknowledged perspective of the organizational structure and dynamics allows us to consistently extrapolate the nature, functionality and added-value of the computer-based tools that constitute the organizational system. The role for information technology is AUGMENTATION.*

Our first objective is to characterize the scenario where organizational computing systems play their parts. This scenario is a broad perspective of the organizational structure and allows us to identify the generic constituents of an organization and their mutual relationships. The identification provides a map of sensitive issues that are prone to the integration of computer-based artifacts, the "hot spots" to be addressed by the systems. These basic notions of organizational structure are presented below. Together with these basic notions, we present an identification of the relations with the organizational computing system, in the context of the technologies and developments proposed by Orchestra.

The view presented here is directly based on Mintzberg's works on organizational structures and dynamics [Mintzberg79, Mintzberg93]. The reason for this choice is that the view presented by Mintzberg was considered as a constructivist perspective on organizations, one that seemed adequate for a comprehensive understanding of how organizations work, providing a clear map for the introduction of technological artifacts. While this may seem as a blind approach to the introduction of technology in organizations, we believe that in no way it hinders the refinement of the purpose of technologies in organizational change. In fact, other approaches to organizational analysis and change like the ones embedded in theories and practices such as TQM [Ross93] or BPR[Hammer93], will use technologies that, in some way, address the components or flows defined by Mintzberg.

The later approaches can be considered as behaviorist perspectives of organizations. While they serve their purpose, a construtivist approach seemed to be better suited for a global reasoning on how information technology could and should impact on the organizational bodies and minds.

The description that follows is a summary of the fundamental concepts of Mintzberg's work[2]. It identifies the main components and the main flows in generic organizations. The taxonomy that Mintzberg proposes for the world of organizations is out of the scope of this report. Along the way, short references entitled "Relation with Orchestra" are included. This is where we hook information technology components and services. The result of this description should be a step by step construction of a set of computer based artifacts and services that cover the different aspects of organizational structure and behavior.

We do not assume the absolute coverage of all organizational aspects with corresponding technologies. Ingenuity, imagination and technological evolution will certainly enable a revision of this design, and the introduction of much more powerful technologies. We only expect the perspective to outlive the technical realization of the Orchestra project.

The Parts of the Organization

A general model for the structure of organizations, according to Mintzberg, includes five basic parts:

- the *operating core* is composed by the operators that carry out the basic activities of the organization like producing products or providing services;
- the *administrative* component, above the *operating core* is composed by *management*, *technostructure* and *support staff*; the *management* component can be further divided in *strategic apex* and the *middle line*. The former is the top of the management hierarchy, the later completes the chain of command down to the *operating core*; the *technostructure* includes the analysts that support the standardization of the work of others and apply analytical techniques to adapt the organization to the environment; and the *support staff* supports the functioning of the organization indirectly. It represents a large component of today's organizations, and includes activities and departments like legal council, payroll or public relations.

The Flows in the Organization

Based on the five part structure, linkages between the parts are defined, which characterizes the organization as a system of flows. This perspective is very significant to the construction of organizational computing systems. If there is room for computer-based support in the organizational environment, it will be correlated with the enhancement of the dynamic behavior of an organization. Furthermore, computer-based support may affect the system of interactions between the parts of an organization and between the individuals that belong to those parts.

---

[2] For a better understanding of these concepts, see referenced works.

Organizations can be viewed according to five different perspectives: as a system of formal authority; as a system of regulated flows; as a system of informal communication; as a system of work constellations; and as a system of ad hoc decision processes.

Formal Authority

The flow of formal authority corresponds to the relations of direct supervision within an organization. It is usually described through the *organizational chart* or *organigram.* Although over simplistic, in the sense that it usually fails to describe the real dynamics of an organization, it reflects the division of labor and identifies: the positions within the organization, the grouping of those positions, and how formal authority flows.

<u>Relation with Orchestra and Organizational Computing Systems</u>

The flow of formal authority defines general rules for the computer-based tools that are specially designed for supervision. It also determines the functionality and operation of the Security and Authentication systems. From the computational description's viewpoint, the flow of formal authority does not raise significant problems. The organigrams are typically hierarchical structures that can be easily captured and described in a computing system.

Regulated Flows

Regulated flows are determined by the standardization of the activities within an organization. Three distinct flows are considered:

- operating work flow;
- flow of control information and decisions;
- and flow of staff information.

Operating work flow includes input, processing and output functions. The input functions receive ``raw" materials or information. Processing reflects a `transformation" process, and the output is the final product delivered by the organization's operating core. *Control Information and Decisions* flow along the hierarchies in a organization. Commands and work instructions flow downwards, while feedback information flows upwards. This feedback information, performance and exceptions, tends to get condensed (aggregated) as it moves upward, and is usually managed by a Management Information System. *Staff Information* consists of reporting relevant facts support specialists, and requesting advice for decision making.

<u>Relation with Orchestra and Organizational Computing Systems</u>

The regulated flows are the most eligible candidates for computer-based support. The *operating workflow* defines the productive functions, goals, deadlines and procedures for a specific activity. In general, this flow is reflected in any computer assisted activity, from manufacturing to banking operations, document publishing, and so on.

The description of the operating work flow is embedded in the computer based tools used by the individuals (or sequences of individuals) in the operating core. This description is the result of task modeling activities and is reflected in the end-user applications.

The control information and decisions flow defines more or less strict protocols between the several levels of the hierarchy. This flow also determines the significant variables to be monitored and the aggregation algorithms that should be applied as the information flows upward. Computer-based tools like communication facilities (for commands and instructions), and Workflow systems play a relevant role in this context.

Control information and decisions can be considered as more or less static social protocols, composed of *indications* and *replies*. The description problems should be addressed in this context, and used to parametrize the Workflow systems to be used.

The staff information flow defines the organization's raw and analytical information. Raw information flows from the middle line to the staff components under the form of facts (sales, new employees, new contracts). These are analyzed for relevance, consistency and completeness by the staff components. Later, this processed information and additional indications coming from the support staff are available for help in decision making, for example. Organizational information bases containing personnel, budgetary, financial or public relations information, should support this flow. The computational description of an organization's raw and analytical information is materialized in a set of information base schemes and manipulation mechanisms.

All the organizational information is contained in a set of heterogeneous, distributed and large scale databases. These databases have to be accessed consistently and integrated in such a way that they form the Organizational Information System to address real world organizations, all the range of databases and hardware platforms (from personal computers to mainframes) has to be considered.

Informal Communication

Authority and regulated flows are not the only mechanisms that shape the dynamics of an organization. Another important contribution is given by informal communication. Informal communication often bypasses established channels for both information access and decision processes. Informal communication is justified on two grounds. First, most activities carried out in modern organizations have a degree of complexity that cannot be fully regulated. Second, organizations are social in nature.

Relation with Orchestra and Organizational Computing Systems
Computer-based systems for informal communication take the form of electronic Mail or Conferencing systems. Interactive tools for person-to-person communication based on advanced multimedia technologies may support richer communication. Information sharing has to be supported in informal communication sessions using the organizational Information System mentioned above.

Work Constellations
Informal communication is often patterned in certain ways. This structuring of the informal communication takes the form of work constellations created due to the aggregation of the individuals. This aggregation occurs according to common hierarchy levels, common productive functions or common temporary goals.

Relation with Orchestra and Organizational Computing Systems
The crystallization of informal and formal communication along work-related or hierarchy-related lines introduces the notions of domain and context in the components of organizational computing systems. A common hierarchy level shapes the communication tools and the shared information base accordingly. A running project creates a specific context for discussion among peers.

The fundamental problem here is the computational description of a *context*. Conferencing tools used currently try to introduce some partition and filtering mechanisms like *Groups* of interest and *Subjects* processing. However, even the static aspects of a context are hard to define. And the dynamics of the work constellations introduce harder problems in the definition and management of a *context*.

Ad Hoc Decision Processes
The last perspective on the dynamics of the organization is the consideration of the *ad hoc decision* processes. A decision process is composed of several phases, that are executed a number of times: the identification phase encompassing problem recognition and problem diagnosis; the development phase including solution search and solution design; the selection phase with solution screening, solution evaluation and choice, and authorization.

Another aspect to consider in the *decision* processes is how they can be categorized. Three kinds of decision processes are identified:

- Operating decisions are performed at the operating core, are largely defined by the regulated flows, and have most of the above phases predetermined.

- Administrative decisions are either coordinated or exceptional. Coordinated administrative decisions are usually regulated, routinely executed by middle line managers or staff members. Exceptional administrative decisions are made at the same level but on an ad hoc basis.
- Strategic decisions have greater impact in the organization. The decision process is obviously more complex, and the several phases require significant effort.

Relation with Orchestra and Organizational Computing Systems

A definition of the decision process is a concept that should be embedded in the components of organizational systems. This concept complements the remaining tools to improve the matching of the system with the organizational structure. The decision must be seen as an autonomous and live entity in the system, with relations to and from the other components.

The phases of the decision processes are usually embedded in tools for decision support. Similar approaches have been adopted for argumentation based systems. Typically, a model of argumentative discourse is adopted. The second aspect that is considered, the categorization of the decision processes, as well as their hierarchy, suggests the notion of composition and dependencies between the elementary decision processes that are run at the multiple levels of the organization.

The above description configures what an organizational system must address or, better stated, the several areas of organizational structures and dynamics where we can design and evaluate information technology enhancements. As stressed above, this is a constructivist view of the world or organizations, and an almost linear extrapolation to the possibilities and challenges of technology.

Perspectives that address specific internal or external behaviors of organizations like, for example, improved organizational learning, total quality management or business process reengineering, must cross their analysis and change approach with the previous organizational perspectives and corresponding technological proposals. If one is to compare the two approaches, breadth is the goal of the former, depth is the goal of the later.

2.2 The Objectives of Orchestra

Besides the conceptual framework presented above, other more pragmatic reasons underlie the definition of the Orchestra project. Previous experience in the development and deployment of office systems shows a recurrent set of limitations:

- office systems are usually islands of automation within the organizations;
- office systems and central information systems are isolated from each other;
- workflow tools, as much as they may already be introduced in the organizational activities, are simply targeted for formal and repetitive processes, being unable to address and manage exceptional conditions;
- existing technology, both at the user or client level or at the system level is too raw and disconnected from the organizational work;
- security and reliability are too limited; communication, decision and negotiation tools are weakly supported by stand-alone and isolated tools.

These observations allow to conclude a set of industrial needs that complement the shape of the Orchestra project:

- The lack of awareness about the organizational structure and dynamics has to be overcome with the inclusion of knowledge and methodologies brought into the project by social sciences and management experts;
- This knowledge and methodologies must be incorporated in the tools provided to the organization, improving their flexibility and support for re-organization decisions
- Office, Workflow and Corporate Information systems must be consistently integrated to provide a seamless interface to the organizational worker
- This integration must go together with the enhancement of the several subsystems, towards a better user environment, and a more secure and open distribution infrastructure
- Communication must be flexible both at the infrastructure level and at the user level, integrating the organizational knowledge mentioned above
- Decision and negotiation tools must be more effective and, above all, not stand-alone, meaning that the overall system will make a proper use of their functionality, in the context of organizational daily work.

The objective of the Orchestra project is:

> To design and develop a Groupware system that increases organizational effectiveness through better management of organizational information, improvement of the communication among individuals and groups, and support to the decision and negotiation processes.

The potential products resulting from Orchestra will then be a toolkit of complementary and integrated technological components and integration expertise that address the multiple dimensions of organizational automation and augmentation through technology, taking into account the intrinsic heterogeneity of large organizations and the existing investments and role of central information systems.

Specific and Measurable Objectives

To achieve the generic goal, the following specific objectives were defined in Orchestra.

1. Normalization of the approach to organizations: to capture the structure and dynamics of an organization, through the use of organizational analysis and diagnosis methodologies. The objective is to harness the methodology, techniques and tools that support the description of the structure and dynamics of an organization. The material result of this activity takes the form of Diagnosis Reports, that are instantiations of the methods and techniques in selected target organizations.

2. Automation of organizational and group work: to build a system for automation of office and organizational work that provides adequate functionality, security and openness for integration with existing IT infrastructures.
2.1. The automation of the organizational procedures is based in interactive computer-supported tools, integrating the office and end-user environments with the workflow management systems. The result is an open system for office activities and seamless integration of workflow, called hereafter User Environment and Workflow Subsystems.
2.2. Data, documents and programs must be manipulated safely, in terms of security and protection assurance. This requires a security system managing authentication of users, client and server programs, in a distributed environment (Security Subsystem).
2.3. The organization's information systems have to be integrated, with provision for global and homogeneous access. This functionality is achieved through the integration of database technology to access and manipulate corporate information systems (Information Subsystem).

3. Effective and Flexible Communication: to provide a powerful communications infrastructure, based on local and wide area networking, supporting traditional data connections, and also audio and video communication. Once the core technology for communication is available, mechanisms for filtering the information dissemination in the organizations are required. This mechanisms optimize the usability and effectiveness of the communication facilities. These two components

are designated hereafter as Communication Subsystem and Communication Filter Subsystem.

4. Better support to informal processes
4.1. To support decision and negotiation. This is done according to two perspectives: quantitative support and qualitative support.
4.2. Quantitative decision support is based on the integration of management and executive information systems that assist in the decision processes, called hereafter Executive Information Subsystem. Qualitative support is provided through the integration of interactive negotiation tools that allow structured interactions among groups, and support the record of those interactions (Negotiation Subsystem).

Criteria for Design and Development. The following yardsticks, or criteria, are implicit in the project goals and strategies, and are proposed for evaluation of the project results:

- Autonomy : Every subsystem of the Orchestra environment is specified, design and implemented, according to the principle of autonomous operation. This requirement is based on the benefits that encapsulation can bring, both to the design and implementation processes, and to the later exploitation of results.
- Conformance to Standards: Every Orchestra subsystem has to conform to the formal or *de facto* standards in the domain it addresses, under realistic assumptions about the evolution of the concerned technologies.
- Generality: The methods and technologies used and integrated in Orchestra are not specific to particular problems, for example concerning the target organizations, but must be generically applicable and extensible.
- Interoperability: Besides clear integration of the several Orchestra subsystems, these must be able to provide some degree of interoperability with existing (both predecessors or co-existing) systems. Interoperability is not defined here as the capability of coordinated integration between multiple Orchestra environments.
- Openness: Every Orchestra subsystem should foresee its own evolution path, allowing integration of new components that optimize efficiency or extend functionality.
- Performance: The Orchestra subsystems are required to have acceptable performance, and comprehensive benchmarking must be provided to quantify performance, identify bottlenecks and allow future improvements.

2.3 A Bit of History

The main approach and definition of the baseline presented above was designed in the Fall of 1992, as it was becoming apparent the fundamental synergy between information technologies and management and organizational trends. The relevance of the topic, from both the research and industrial viewpoints, suggested the instantiation of a project that could bootstrap a significant effort in the area of Organizational Computing. This was the seed idea for the Orchestra project.

2.3.1 The Initial Consortium and Proposal

The opportunity of the 1993 Esprit Call, which deadline was scheduled for April, motivated the search for a consortium and the preparation of a proposal. The main guidelines for the build up of the Orchestra consortium were the following:

- A consistent, manageable and synergistic **industrial core**, with internal commercial relations and with an installed market base. This concept led to the choice of SMD Informatica, and Novabase, two companies of the AITEC[3] group, spin offs of the INESC activities. SMD Informatica had decided that the evolution of its office product Elenix Multimedia should address the issues of workflow, security and corporate systems integration.

Software AG was identified as an interesting partner, both for its very significant share of the mainframe market and its competence in information systems and communication technologies, ranging from mainframe systems to personal computers. Moreover, the Spanish branch of Software AG had a significant share of the Iberian market, together with good relations with the other southern European and southern American markets.

Lisle was a small company, located in Madrid, specifically devoted to representation, servicing and dissemination of products originating from the AITEC universe, and also to the marketing of technologies.

- A complementary competence in the **research and development** aspects of Orchestra, namely organizational analysis, security, intelligent or contextual

[3] AITEC is an organization that supports the creation of spin-off companies emerging from the activities of INESC and manages participations in these (as well as other) type of companies (Information Technology and Electronics).

communication and interactive decision and negotiation tools. INESC was an obvious partner for these areas and UPM (Universidad Politecnica de Madrid) showed its interest and ability to provide significant contributions. The expertise required for the fundamental step that consisted of the organizational diagnosis (methodologies for and execution of the information gathering processes) was sought at a management and sociology school, ISCTE/INDEG.

- The users, or in the Orchestra case, **the pilots**, were defined as small sized organizations, or sub-organizations, which role was: (1) to provide information and the context of real world organizations; (2) to install the base technology (Elenix & Software AG components mainly); and (3) to use, as much as possible, the early prototypes developed in the project, with the aim of assessing the impact of the use of these technologies in the work environments.

The user or pilot organizations invited into the consortium were:
EDP - Electricidade de Portugal, S.A. is one of the largest portuguese companies. EDP is devoted to the supplying, transmission and distribution of electrical energy. The key area chosen for the piloting of the Orchestra system was the Thermal Power Plant of Sines. The Sines Power Plant includes around 270 workers and a choice of specific departments had to be made to integrate the Orchestra results. Further relations within the prospective Orchestra consortium included the fact that EDP was the main customer of Software AG in Portugal. Together with EDP, the consortium also included Edinfor - Sistemas Informáticos, S.A.. Edinfor was fully controlled by EDP, and acted as a subsidiary company whose aim was to manage all the EDP database structures and to supply technical support and services. EDINFOR has knowledge in "Facilities Management" overviewing the development of automatic integrated systems within the field of both services and industrial companies. The situation of EDP and Edinfor evolved during the project, and resulted in the splitting of EDP in a set of regional and vertical companies, and the transformation of EDP in a holding organization[4].

CN (Comunicações Nacionais), in Lisbon, Portugal, was a holding that managed the Public participations in the major telecommunication operators in Portugal (Telecom, TLP (Telefones de Lisboa e Porto), Marconi, TDP). The role of Comunicacoes Nacionais was to coordinate the activities and relations of the several companies of the holding; CN was a small organization of around 30 people, charged with strategic planning and decision making. In the context of the project, CN was also a close partner to INESC since the shareholders structure of INESC included the telecommunication operators. This description is presented in the past tense since, as we will see below, the evolution of the telecommunications

[4] Later in the project, Edinfor made a proposal to become a "testbed" for some of the Orchestra prototypes, which was accepted by the Consortium.

sector in Portugal led to the shut down of Comunicações Nacionais in the Summer of 1995.

UITESA, in Madrid, Spain, focuses its activities on technological consulting and advanced engineering services. For this it combines analysis of productive processes (such as physical phenomena simulation, reliability models and resources optimization, among others) and integration of operating support technologies (on line information systems, telecontrol, etc). UITESA is entirely owned by H.I. Holding (IBERDROLA Industrial Group) and is the leading company in the area of engineering and, thus, actively participates in the Group's diversification policy. IBERDROLA is an investor owned electric utility in Spain that generates, transmits and delivers electric power to almost 8 million customers. The organization which ended up being chosen[5] as the Orchestra pilot was CONUC (Combustible Nuclear), a small organization of engineers and physicists charged with the management and acquisition of nuclear fuel for the Iberdrola nuclear powerplants.

Table 1. List of initial Orchestra partners

Partner	Country	Role
INESC	Portugal	Coordinating
Software AG	Germany/Spain	Partner
EDP	Portugal	Partner
UITESA	Portugal	Partner
CN	Portugal	Partner
SMD	Portugal	Associated to INESC
Novabase	Portugal	Associated to INESC
Edinfor	Portugal	Associated to EDP
Univ Politecnica Madrid	Spain	Associated to Uitesa
ISCTE/INDEG	Portugal	Associated to INESC
Lisle	Spain	Associated to Uitesa

To summarize, by **April 22nd of 1993**, a proposal was presented to the European Commission, DG XII, Esprit Programme, Advanced Home and Business Systems, with the above eleven (11) organizations as members of the consortium, made up of five (5) partners and six (6) associated partners (see table above).

[5] Much later in the timeframe of the project. Once the project was approved, an initial phase was dedicated to the search and choice of the actual pilot organizations.

The total effort requested in the initial proposal was **106 person*years**, for a duration of 3 years or 36 months. This configuration led to a total projected cost of 15791 Ecu, and a corresponding request for **funding of 7895 KECU**

2.3.2 Proposal Revision and Final Configuration

The negotiation of the proposal took place between June 1993 and January 1994. The main facts were the following:

- After the submission and the evaluation process, the project was considered as viable for acceptance, with a maximum budget (cost) of around 7500 KECU, and a suggestion of a reduction to a 24 month or 2 year duration.
- After several meetings in Brussels, that aimed at conciliating the project structure and goals with the Programme charter and with other proposals that had been submitted. The meetings took place in June, September and November. In December 1993, the request for a Technical Annex was issued by the European Commission and led to the production of an initial version in January 1994. This technical annex reflected some fundamental changes:

(1) a significant part of the work related with the design and development of organizational analysis tools was dropped;
(2) a significant part of the Software AG effort was moved from Germany to Spain, thus lowering the budget associated with manpower;
(3) the objectives of several tasks were downgraded in order to be feasible in the new duration of 2 years.

- The resulting technical annex showed a total effort of **54.3 person*years** and a total cost of 7101 KEcu, with a corresponding **request for funding of 3551 KECU.**

The next step was a minor change introduced by the suggestion (originally made by the EC officers) of integrating Taskon, a Norwegian company devoted to the design, development, and exploitation of object oriented software tools and methodologies. The integration of Taskon should complement the efforts in the area of computer support to organizational analysis and was welcome in the project. Its integration suggested the definition of another pilot, close to Taskon, so that the use of Taskon tools for the purpose of organizational analysis (workflow modeling in particular) could be evaluated in an easier way. This Norwegian pilot was suggested but its Integration on the project was suspended. Further modifications to the initial structure included the upgrade of the status of SMD and Novabase to the role of partner (instead of associated partner as proposed). This resulted in a total of eight (8) partners and four (4) associated partners (see Table 2).

Table 2. List of Final Orchestra Partners

Partner	Country	Role
INESC	Portugal	Coordinating
SMD	Portugal	Partner
Novabase	Portugal	Partner
Software AG	Germany/Spain	Partner
Taskon	Norway	Partner
EDP	Portugal	Partner
UITESA	Portugal	Partner
CN	Portugal	Partner
Edinfor	Portugal	Associated to EDP
Univ Politecnica Madrid	Spain	Associated to Uitesa
ISCTE/INDEG	Portugal	Associated to INESC
Lisle	Spain	Associated to Uitesa

The final version of the Technical Annex, including the full set of partners and associated partners, tasks and resources, was therefore delivered in March 1994 (official date of the Technical Annex Document is March 25th, 1994). The project, named Orchestra, and classified as ESPRIT project 8794, was created. The official starting date was defined to be June 1st 1994, 20 months after the conceptual foundations were designed [6].

[6] Just as a word of advice to readers interested in setting up a project like this: June is the worst possible month to start a project. Holidays happen in July in most northern European countries, and August is a shutdown month for southern European countries. The consequence is that, after some meetings in June, nothing real happens until September and a consistent delay of two months propagates throughout the project.

3. Functionality of the Orchestra Environment

A global map of the functionality provided by the Orchestra components is presented in this chapter. The organizational keyword of the Orchestra project imposes an extended notion of the word functionality to encompass a methodological component, rather than a strictly technical perspective. In fact, the functionality of a given technical component can not be dissociated from a process of integration of that component in an organizational environment. Basically, most of the components of an organizational system require the gathering and classification of organizational information, a requirement that is specifically related with most of the Orchestra components (the awareness keyword in Orchestra).

Once organizational information is gathered and made available in some computerized and analyzable format, it can be used by run time components to provide services to the users of the organizational system. The description of the functionality defined and provided by the Orchestra system follows the big picture presented in the previous chapter, and consolidate in four main areas of services:

- The organizational analysis itself, as a computer supported process designed to achieve a comprehensive description of the organization namely, as we will see, the work procedures.
- The run time elements that interact with the user, usually classified as the office environment, and that automate regulated procedures, known as the workflow system. In this scope, we also include two fundamental components of the technological framework, the security facilities, and the mainframe or legacy systems integration.
- The communication facilities destined to support and enhance the interpersonal and inter-group communication, address the informal communication flows mentioned in chapter 2.
- Tools for quantitative and qualitative decision making are the fourth area of functionality and are meant to enhance the ad hoc decision processes that occur in any organization.

The functionality and approaches described in this report are the ones actually provided by the final prototypes of the Orchestra project. While they do not diverge radically from the initial goals (stated in the **Proposal** and **Technical**

Annex), there are obvious shifts of emphasis and particular aspects that deserve attention, justifying a global perspective at this stage.

3.1 Organizational Analysis

The process of gathering and classification of organizational information, henceforth designated as organizational analysis, must be seen as an Orchestra functionality itself. This functionality is a complex process involving the methodology and process of information gathering. and the supporting analysis technologies (modeling tools). The initial process concerns the gathering of information in the target organizations. In the case of Orchestra, several pilot organizations were included. A major issue in this phase is the choice of the methodology for organizational analysis, and this aspect will be discussed next.

After the gathering of information, the organizational modeling proceeds with the aid of computer-based tools. In the case of Orchestra, a particular emphasis was put on the modeling workflow procedure, in particular because this process would have direct impact on the use/feed of the run time components like the workflow engine. Also, a particular tool was used, Taskon's OORAM, which resulted in a set of advantages and unavoidable limitations, which will be mentioned below and referred to in additional documents.

3.1.1 Analysis Methodology and Information Gathering[7]

The task of organizational analysis was undertaken in Orchestra by ISCTE/INDEG, a social sciences school. This section presents the fundamental approach used in the analytical work performed at the pilots: Comunicações Nacionais (CN), Electricidade de Portugal (EDP) - Central Termoeléctrica de Sines (CTS) e Iberdrola (CONUC).

3.1.1.1 Which Approach to Organizational Diagnosis?

The organizational analysis must be based on concrete assumptions regarding the nature, work and structure of the organizations (Daft and Weick, 1984). These assumptions play the following roles:

- They allow the identification of the relevant elements from the set of information that can be obtained about an organization;

[7] Description based on deliverable 1.1.1 - Diagnosis Methodology, authored by ISCTE/INDEG. The analysis work was done in collaboration with the teams in the pilots. At EDP-CTS, it also had the participation of Edinfor. At CONUC, UITESA supported this work.

- They assign a meaning to the relevant elements for a given objective;
- They allow the establishment of relationships between that elements, and, through these relations, explain the organization's reality;
- They function as a basis to forecast the future state of the organizations.

For the analytical work these assumptions can be only implicit, without being less operative, as they are the reference benchmark used by the analyst. As Morgan (1986) states, the benchmarks suited for organizational analysis are multiple and show advantages and drawbacks. Thus, the execution of a specific diagnosis must be guided by one or more models suited for that problem. It is useful to explain the model(s) used, since this allows us to be aware of the advantages and disadvantages of the approach. In Orchestra, four factors had influence on the choice of an approach to the diagnosis:

1. The Organizational nature of the pilots. Previous knowledge about the pilot organizations activities, allowed us expect a clear differentiation both in structures and in organizational processes. For instance, CN (Comunicações Nacionais) was a holding company with responsibilities at the strategic level while EDP-CTS (Central Termoeléctrica de Sines) is an energy production unit. This reality suggested the use of a model that would be sufficiently open, in order to deal with this diversity.
2. Level and type of change required by the pilots. After the first contact with the pilots, it was obvious to verify that they were not interested in undertaking a process of radical change, as it is could be suggested, for example, by a business process reengineering approach. On the other hand, it was clear from the beginning that, for the specific case of CTS, Orchestra would not focus on the whole organization, but only on the Administrative Department.
3. Tools for organizational analysis. Orchestra assumed the use of TASKON/OORAM methodology (see below). According to this methodology, the world is defined through role models, describing information flows between the different roles. A mapping between several models and administrative processes in an organization can be easily understood. The emphasis on gathering workflow procedures was therefore clear from the beginning. To gather information and communication flows, we used work analysis methods and process models. The later agrees with Total Quality perspective, where the collection of information on inputs, transformation and outputs, allows the definition of improvements to the processes without undertaking major changes.
4. Scope of Orchestra. Given the global approach to organizational dynamics, the diagnosis approach had to encompass both formal and informal aspects of the organization, and therefore a model that included variables related with these aspects had to be found.

Considering the above requirements, the ISCTE's team opted for the model developed by Porras (1987), called Stream Analysis. The reasons for this choice were:

- The Stream Analysis is capable of integrating variables of very distinct nature, such as organizational and social aspects, technology and space, which matched the Orchestra requirements
- The Stream Analysis model is an open model, concerning data collection techniques, allows a smooth integration with the TASKON methodology in the areas of description of the administrative systems and/or work flow design.
- The Stream Analysis model provides a conceptual methodology for organizational change which is consistent with the organizational analysis process. This allows for more integrated intervention plans. This consistency supported the introduction of new work procedures in the pilots.

Figure 3-1. Stream Organization Model (Porras, 1987)

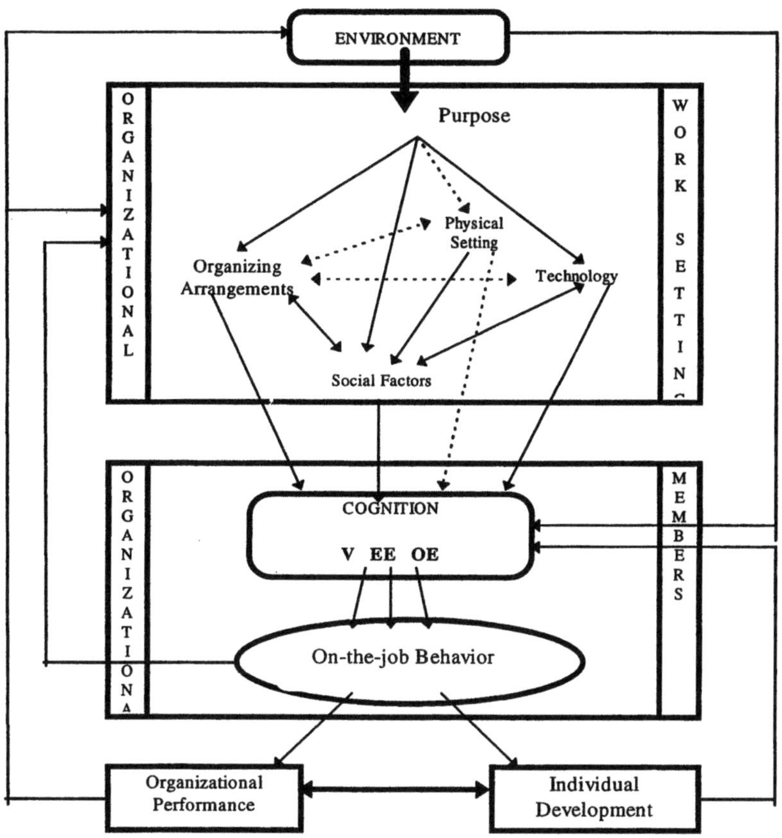

3.1.1.2 The Basic Analytical Model: Stream Analysis

The Stream Analysis Model was developed by Porras (1987) and is based on the organizational concept illustrated in the next figure. We enumerate the key elements of the model: Organizing Arrangements, Technology, Social Factors, and Physical Settings. A refinement of these is presented in Figure 3-2.

Figure 3-2. Description of Organizational Components in the Stream Organization Model (Porras 1987)

1. Org. Arrangements	**2. Social factors**	**3. Technology**	**4. Physical Settings**
A. Goals	A. Culture Basic Assumptions, Values, Norms, Language and jargon, Rituals, History, Stories, Myths, Symbols	A. Tools, Equipment, and Machinery	A. Space Configuration Size, Shape, Relative Locations
B. Strategies	B. Interaction Processes Interpersonal, Group, Intergroup	B. Technical Expertise	B. Physical Ambiance Light, Heat, Noise, Air Quality, Cleanliness
C. Formal Structure	C. Social patterns and networks Communication, Problem solving and decision making, Influence, Status	C. Job Design	C. Interior Design Decoration, Furniture, Window Covering, Floor Coverings, Colors
D. Administrative Policies and Procedures	D. Individual Attributes Attitudes and beliefs, Behavioral Skills, Feelings	D. Work Flow Design	D. Architectural Design
E. Administrative Systems		E. Technical Policies and Procedures	
F. Formal reward Systems Evaluation System, Pay Systems, Benefits Packages		F. Technical Systems	

3.1.1.3 The Analysis Methodology

The data collection process was based on semi-directive interviews to the key elements of the organizational units and processes under analysis. The main characteristic of this type of interview is the existence of a guideline and a set of topics to be treated. This guideline although not rigid, allows the collection of information equally adequate to the objective of our work.

The interview focused mainly on the purposes and responsibilities of each department or area of the organization under analysis. From this information, the work and communication flows were captured, bearing in mind the model of the process. From the communicational flows some critical incidents and the potential resistance to provision of information of this incidents were diagnosed.

Steps of the Process of Collecting Data. As mentioned above, the instantiation of the analysis process at EDP-CTS included two distinct steps. In a first step, the organization as a whole was analyzed, departments and functions were identified, and interaction patterns among organizational units were understood. The starting point of this analysis were direct interviews to the Heads of three departments- Administrative, Conduction and Maintenance - and also to the persons in charge of the two main areas that related to Maintenance- Electrical and Mechanical/Boiler. The second step focused on the Administrative Department. Its various areas were analyzed: bookkeeping, personnel, treasury, secretariat, storehouse, stocks, provision, stewardship. In each of these areas one or more of its workers was interviewed.

In CN, the process of collecting data was done in another way, given that the organization had different characteristics of the Central de Sines. The interviews were done to the responsible of the denominated Staff of decisional support (computing, juridical, management and financial coordination, strategically planning) and to do Direction of the Administrative Services. A similar process was carried out at CONUC, Iberdrola, Madrid, Spain.

The chapter entitled "The Pilots" summarizes these descriptions of the pilots in terms of these organizational components. Some aspects were left out of this report (for example, the Physical Settings), since they were considered as not very relevant to the designs and developments of Orchestra.

Sources of Information

- Document analysis
  CN - SIG's report and report of consolidated accounts
  EDP-CTS - Administrative Department and Storehouse Manuals
- Analysis of Critical incidents: The application of the later method was meant to identify which information flow were seen as cause of trouble and to

anticipate some of the justifications of that trouble. Crisp and clear answers in this domain proved to be hard to obtain, since the question clearly raised fears and concerns in the interviewed. Despite this resistance, significant failures in some processes could be detected. The analysis of these failures in the organizational flows can be fundamental to evaluate the impact of the Orchestra system in the target environment.

3.1.1.4 A Comment on the Analysis Results

The results of the organizational analysis performed in the initial phase of the Orchestra project have been subject to some criticism both within the consortium and outside it (during the review processes). The main concerns were essentially its decoupling from business or macroscopic organizational processes. In fact, this happens fundamentally due to the analytical model that was adopted. The results can be classified into two major groups:

- High level descriptions of organizational components (some, not all),
- and low level descriptions of micro processes.

After the experience in Orchestra, it is fair to say that this result is probably the only one might expect in the project with the scope and configuration of Orchestra. First, the approach was centered on the observation of organizations with the purpose of designing adequate technology. No change requirements, intentions, or plans have been expressed by the target organizations. On the other hand, the broad coverage of the Orchestra technologies required, as mentioned above, a sufficiently broad analytical model. An argument against this choice, which is acceptable, is that the result of the analysis is too vague to be directly useful in technology design, implementation and deployment. An argument for this choice is that analysis methodologies directed to business processes are only targeted to effective integration of worflow technologies, thus leaving behind other relevant dimensions like informal communication or ad hoc decision processes.

A retrospective view on the analysis process suggests that some middle level analysis, between the high level descriptions suggested by the Stream Organizational Model, and the micro processes, encompassing macroscopic processes should have deserved more attention. It should be noted that some composite processes have been assembled based on the capture of the microprocesses. These composite processes are however very much local to organizational units and often do not traverse the organization.

3.1.2 Computer-based Modeling [8]

The ORCHESTRA project approached the problem of modeling workflow in the larger scope of organizational description and modeling. To support organizational modeling in general, and workflow modeling in particular, we decided to use Taskon OORAM (*Object Oriented Role Analysis and Modeling*) [Reenskaug96].

The OORAM tool was applied in the analysis of four different pilot organizations, mentioned in the previous sections and described with more detail in a subsequent chapter.

- Pilot 1 is the administrative department of a thermal powerplant with a dozen users (EDP-CTS, Sines, Portugal).
- Pilot 2 is a holding company with strategic functions and around 30 members (CN, Lisbon, Portugal).
- Pilot 3 is a small organization of physicists and engineers that manages the nuclear fuel orders for Spanish nuclear powerplants (CONUC, Iberdrola, Madrid, Spain).
- Pilot 4 is a testbed laboratory in Norway, sponsored by several large Norwegian companies (BEST program).

Most of the flows collected by the ISCTE/INDEG team, for the Pilots 1, 2, and 3 are represented in the above mentioned WWW pages. Pilot 4 was used for a comparative analysis of workflow modeling techniques (OORAM, Staffware, Action), and the fundamental conclusions are described in deliverable D 5.4.3 [9], and summarized below.

3.1.2.1 Experience in Modeling [10]

After the data collection in each pilot organization, workflows were modeled using the Taskon/OORAM methodology. The objective of this process was to improve

---

[8] Description based on deliverables D1.3.1, Taskon/OORAM integration, authored by Jørn Andersen, Taskon A/S, Deliverables 1.1.2 - Diagnosis of Target Organizations, authored by Luís Reto and Albino Lopes, ISCTE/INDEG (appendices with OORAM models authored by Ana Paula Pereira, INESC), Deliverable 5.4.3, Workflow modeling in the Norwegian BEST Pilots, authored by Babak Farshchain, P.-H. Carlsen, NTH/Taskon A/S, Deliverables 5.4.5, 5.4.6, which include the modeling results from BEST pilots (Fokus and Statoil), and information available on the Web, http://amadeus.inesc.pt./tim/projects/modeling/

[9] Deliverable 5.4.3, Workflow modeling in the Norwegian BEST Pilots, authored by Babak Farshchain, P.-H. Carlsen, NTH/Taskon A/S

[10] For complete information and exhaustive diagrams, see Orchestra Deliverables 1.1.2, which include the modeling results for the three initial pilots (CN, EDP-CTS, and CONUC) and Deliverables 5.4.5, 5.4.6, which include the modeling results from BEST pilots (Fokus and Statoil). An other report exists related with another pilot organization. However, its modeling results have been considered as confidential.

the understanding of the work processes through a description in a common model. According to the OORAM methodology this was done in three iterative steps:

1. Definition of which parts of the organization's environment should be considered, including identification of information to be manipulated, system borders and interfaces to existing systems.
2. Identification and analysis of the major actors. For each one, information about tasks, information's needs and results, goals, responsibilities and collaborators must be defined.
3. Identification and modeling of the major organizational processes that will have relations or impact on the ORCHESTRA subsystems. Within the area of concern of each work process, a role model was created focusing on the following views: collaboration, scenario and process view. This stage clarifies roles, identifies activities and actions, defines information flows and alternative process courses, and defines the mappings from actor to role.

The Taskon/OORAM Tool and Approach

TASKON/OORAM is based on a pure object-oriented concept. Role models are the central construct. A role model describes how objects collaborate in a structure in order to perform some function of the overall system.

In role models, objects are like clerks in an organization: they are organized in a structure of collaboration, where each clerk or object has its own responsibility within the organization. A clerk has a position in the organization, an object plays one or more roles in the object's structure. A clerk has a certain competence which makes him qualified to fill one or more positions, an object has a type that gives it the behavior it needs to play one or more roles. The task of the organizational consultant is to create an effective work organization, the task of the system designer is to create an effective role model that organizes the system's objects in an effective way. In another analogy one may think of a role model as a certain act in a play. The actors collaborate in a certain structure to perform properly. The identity of the actor is not important as long as he/she fulfill the specific requirements of the role.

Systems of interacting objects may have different views, each one expressing certain aspects of the system of roles while suppressing others. OORAM analysis supports several views on the role model, four of which where used for making the System User Model of each pilot organization. This model allows us to understand the system context and selected work processes in each organization:

- Area of Concern View - Free text describing the phenomenon modeled by the role model.
- Collaboration View - Shows the roles and the message paths between them.
- Scenario View - Describes specific, time ordered sequences of interactions between objects.
- Process View - Describes data flow between roles and actions taken by roles to process the data.

Figure 3-3 - Collaboration View of an OORAM Role Model

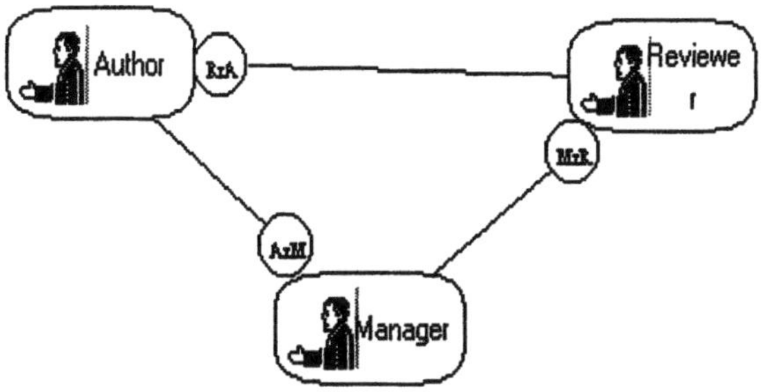

Figure 3-4 - Scenario View of an OORAM Role Model

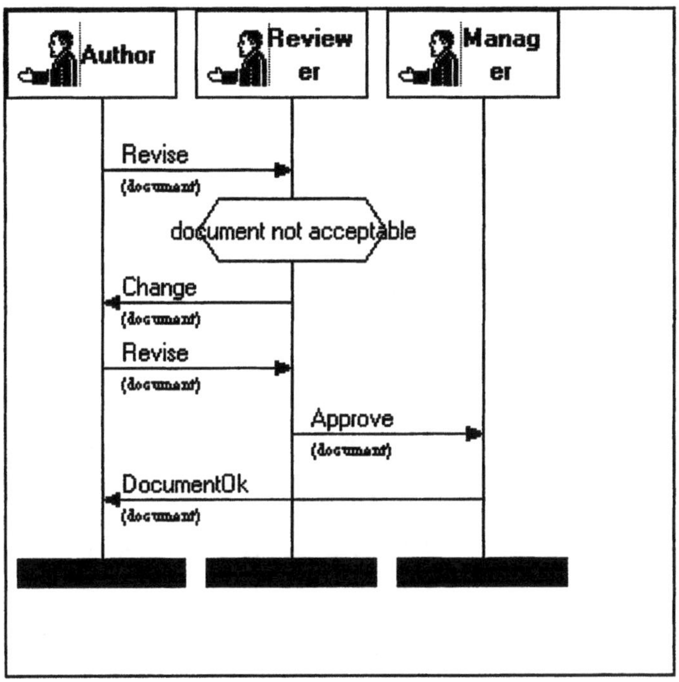

Figure 3-5 - Process View of an OORAM Role Model

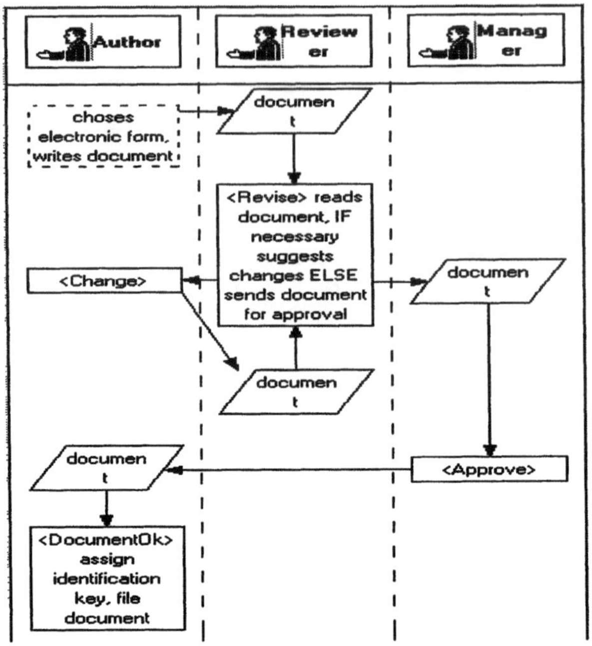

Figure 3-6 - From process view to System Model

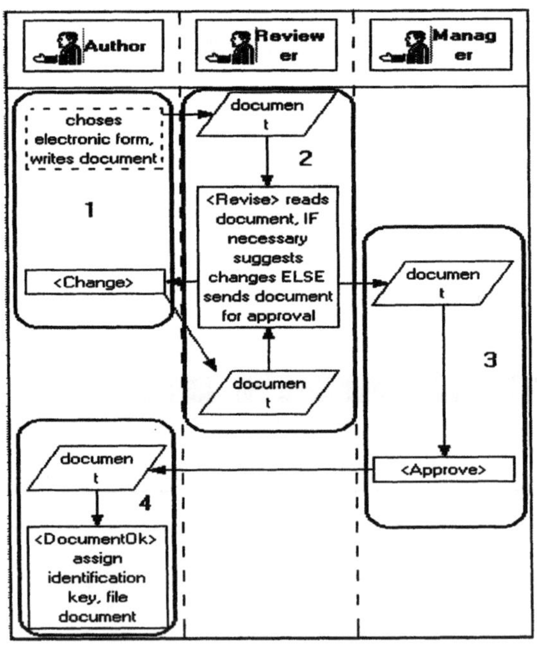

Figure 3-7 - Requirements Model in OORAM

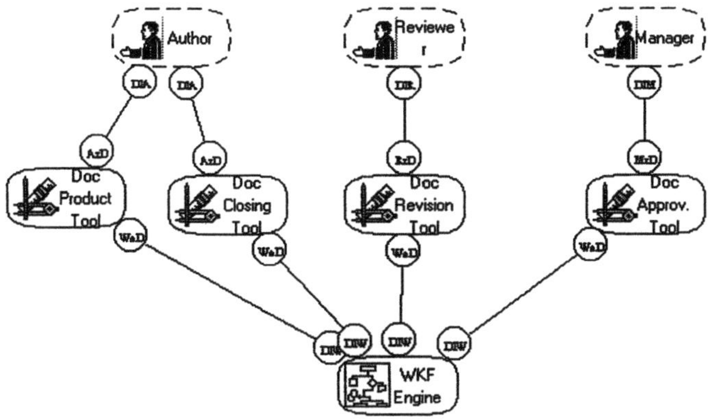

The list below shows which type of flows and OORAM role models were captured. The examples come from the flows of EDP Sines Thermal Powerplant.

Management of Proposals
Request for services; Generic proposals reception; Specific proposals reception; Scheduling proposals opening; Proposals adjudication; Answering suppliers;
Personnel Management
Extra allowance; Extratime authorization; Extratime registration; Luncheon vouchers request (extratime); Luncheon vouchers request; Luncheon vouchers nullified;
Transports Management
Request repair under 50000 PTE;Repair payment under 50000 PTE; Request repair above 50000 PTE; Repair payment above 50000 PTE; Repair proposals opening and adjudication; Car accident participation ;Taxicab payment
Medical Expenses
Refunding medical expenses - convened doctors; Refunding medical expenses - non convened doctors; Payment of medical expenses; Meal subsidy deduction
Steward Tasks
Steward restocking request; Material request to steward; Tool request; Tool replacement
Storehouse product Management
Storehouse products entrance; Storehouse products request; Analysis and control of deviations; Stock programming and controlling
Treasury
Treasury reinforcement; Advancement for urgent purchases; Monthly control of advancements
Bookkeeping
General invoice control; Debit/Credit note control
Bureau
Sending a fax

3.1.2.2 OORAM versus Existing Workflow Tools[11]

The use of OORAM modeling tools as the approach for capturing Workflow Information has specific advantages and drawbacks. The modeling experience reported by Taskon was done together with a comparative analysis with other commercial systems, specifically Staffware and Action.

The approach was to apply OORAM and the above commercial workflow management systems to three industrial real cases. This effort highlighted the most significant aspects of using OORAM for workflow modeling, both with regard to the workflow aspects in general and also with regard to the state of the art within the field. The pilot modeling resulted in a set of generic requirements to workflow modeling, used in an evaluation of OORAM used in workflow modeling. Last, but not least, some suggestions for improvements and further development of OORAM related to workflow were extracted. This approach also provided the opportunity to compare OORAM with the commercial workflow systems. In the framework of the derived workflow requirements this was performed in a checklist form. In addition, a survey of available workflow management systems has been performed in order to give a more complete picture of the field.

The Orchestra pilot 4 involved three major Norwegian companies: Fokus Bank, Statoil Data and Uni Storebrand. Each of the companies provided a real case from their businesses which has been consider as a crucial and relevant application for workflow system development. The pilot cases were of different character. The Fokus bank is a typical banking process, while Uni Storebrand presented a typical insurance process. The Statoil Data case is the handling of project prospects[12].

After the comparative modeling process, the final evaluation can be summarized in the following statements:

On OORAM :

- At the present stage, no special workflow related features are included. It neither includes a workflow runtime environment nor bridges to external workflow engines. OORAM only supports transition to general implementation environments as Smalltalk and C++. Further, typical workflow aspects as e.g. timing and deadlines must be modeled and analyzed "manually". Therefore the advantages of OORAM are in the analysis and design phases of a workflow system development. As OORAM is strictly object oriented, it captures the essence of this technology:
    - modeling based on patterns of interacting objects,

[11] This short description is based on Taskon's deliverable D 5.4.3, referred to above.
[12] See detailed description of cases in Deliverables 5.4.4 to 5.4.5

- supporting both data-centered and process-centered approaches on the same model,
- mastering the complexity by separation of concern and model inheritance,
- building large models/systems through systematic application of reusable components.

- The technology foundations of OORAM shows a great potential for modeling of business processes where process data and tasks are closely related.

On Staffware :

- In many ways Staffware is the total opposite of OORAM. Staffware is more of a workflow development than a workflow modeling system, a specialized workflow for workflow applications. It is process oriented and the methodology is based on sending data around an organization. The advantage of Staffware is the set of support functions (as e.g. facilities for integration with external systems) and the integrated implementation environment, including a runtime environment on a client-server architecture.
- The process definition is very rigid. There are no abstraction mechanisms for aggregation of processes and tasks. Furthermore, separate workflows have no possibilities to cooperate with each other and the possibilities to divide complex processes in more simple ones are limited. Therefore, process definitions become large and complex. Support for reuse is weak, and limited to traditional copy-paste functions.
- The organizational aspects are totally ignored in Staffware as there are no process analysis facilities included.

On Action Technologies

- Action Technologies is the most complete workflow management system of the three. It includes an analysis module, the Action Analyst, to model and analyze the models which is a graphical easy-to-use tool. There is no independent workflow runtime integrated in the tool, but there is a workflow builder and runtime environment available for Lotus Notes.
- The methodology is based on the speech-act theory where a workflow is modeled as a commitment between the provider and the customer of a service. Each process is a hierarchy of such commitments. The modeling language is quite simple, but it is difficult to understand the concept of commitments and conversations/dialogues. When the analyst is familiar with the modeling concept, the method is quite suitable for BPR analysis. However, it is not always simple to model all types of tasks as dialogues.
- Analogue to Staffware there is very limited potential for advanced reuse.

Together with these general comments, an evaluation framework was proposed, including evaluation criteria and indices that we list below. To see how the compared systems rate under this evaluation framework, please look at the reports D.5.4.3.

Method/Tool related requirements

- Executeability, Reducibility, Changeability,
- Analyzability, Integration, Modularity/Reuse

Language dependent requirements

- Perceptibility, Expressive power, Expressive economy

Workflow applicability

- Workflow environment completeness
- Environment upgradeability
- Confidence/commitment in developing organization

3.1.2.3 From OORAM Models to Workflow Enactment

The Orchestra workflow tool (see next section on User Environment and Workflow system) and OORAM have two different approaches to model workflow in an organization. The Orchestra workflow tool's way of doing it is to describe the workflow in a Petri-net and give detailed information to what happens in each node and between the nodes. The workflow model becomes very compact, and all information essential to the workflow is visualized together. The drawback is that it can be difficult to read and understand such compact models because all the information is bundled together. The identification of interesting information elements may be hard because, to use an old analogy, you cannot see the forest because of the trees.

OORAM has a different approach to workflow modeling. In OORAM, different aspects of the workflow model are modeled into a huge comprehensive model, but which one can only see one aspect at a time. These are the *aspect views*. Different views on a model allows to easily focus on different aspects of the workflow model and model them correctly. In OORAM one has a divide and conquer philosophy. When we have modeled and understood the different aspects of the workflow model, we will have a complete description of the workflow model. If we use the analogy above one can say that we have found the trees individually and by that got a full description of the forest.

The mapping from OORAM models to workflow enactment can be looked at as a mapping at different levels. The figure below describes four levels of mapping:

- **The Concept Layer** describes the conceptual mapping the two environments.
- **The Transfer Layer** where the wanted OORAM information may be extracted into an OORAM datamodel.
- **The Datamodel Layer** decribes datamodels for OORAM and the Workflow tool.
- **The Physical Database Layer** is the physical implementation layer.

Figure 3-8 - OORAM and Workflow Engine Mapping

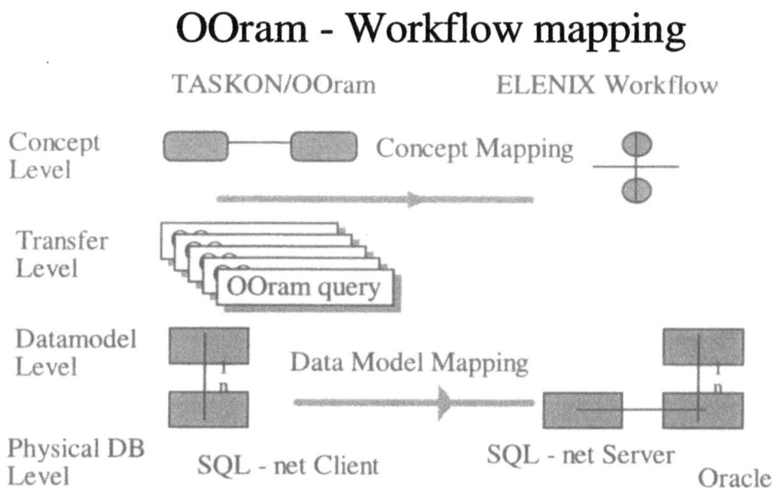

Mapping at the Concept Level. To better understand the different approaches to workflow modeling we will look at an example. The example will illustrate the similarities and the differences between the modeling techniques regarding concepts and model elements. The example is to model how an employee in the organization fills a report describing the personal expenses the employee had during a project. The expense report is approved or rejected by the employee's department manager. On approval the department manager will send the report to the account manager in the organization as an invoice. The account manager will finally (hopefully) send some money to the employee.

We assume that the elements and concepts in the figure above are known. In OORAM one model different aspects of the workflow model, and in the figures below you can see the different aspects of a workflow model described in OORAM.

By using OORAM to find the roles, one will end with roles described in the collaboration view above. In the Orchestra workflow tool example there was a role with the name **No Role**. In OORAM there exist no **No Roles**. Every role in OORAM describes a function an object plays in an area of concern, i.e. every role has a purpose. In OORAM one identify what is outside the system and what is inside the system. Roles outside the system either trigger a stimulus and/or receive a response from the system. In this example we have identified a Report requester and Archivist is outside the system.

Figure 3-9 -The example in Orchestra's workflow tool model

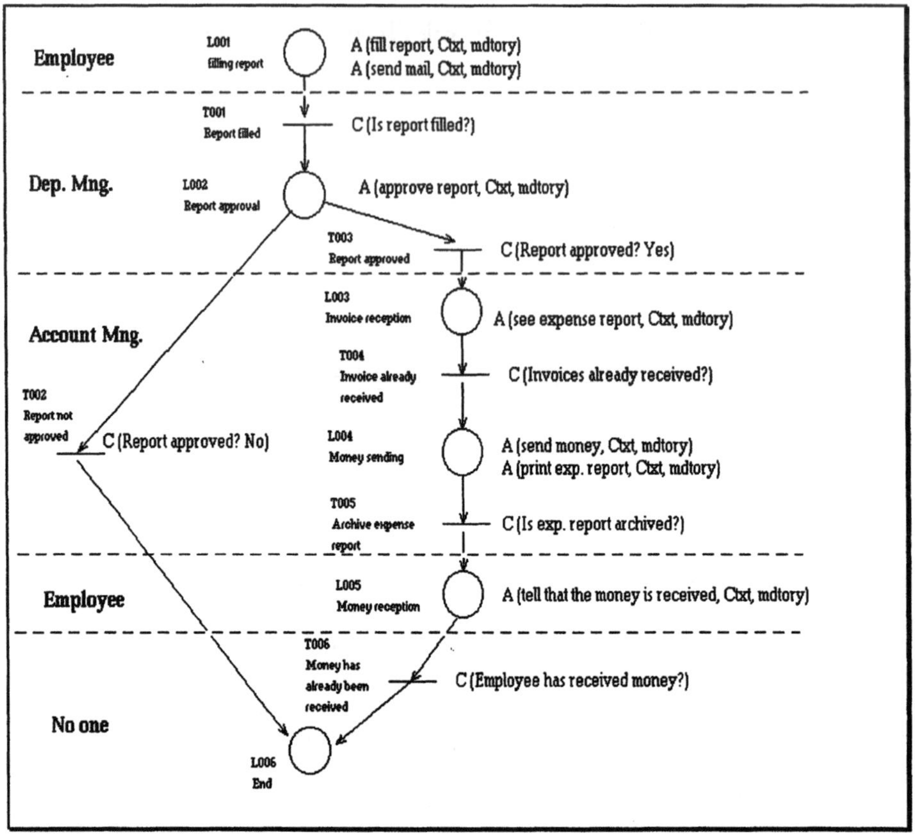

Figure 3-10 -The collaboration view

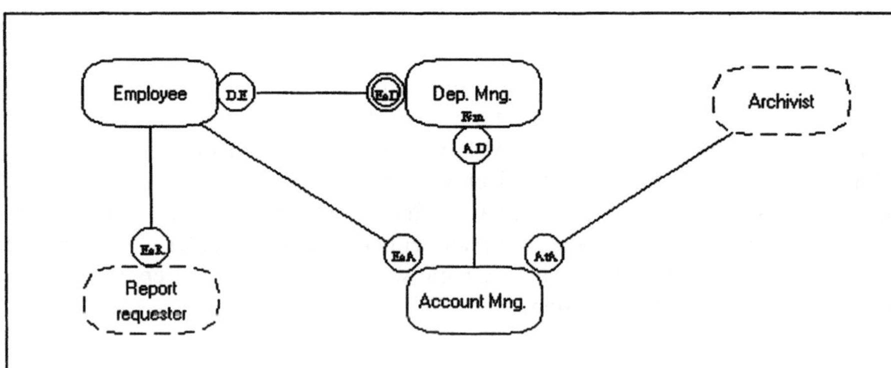

Figure 3-11 - The process view

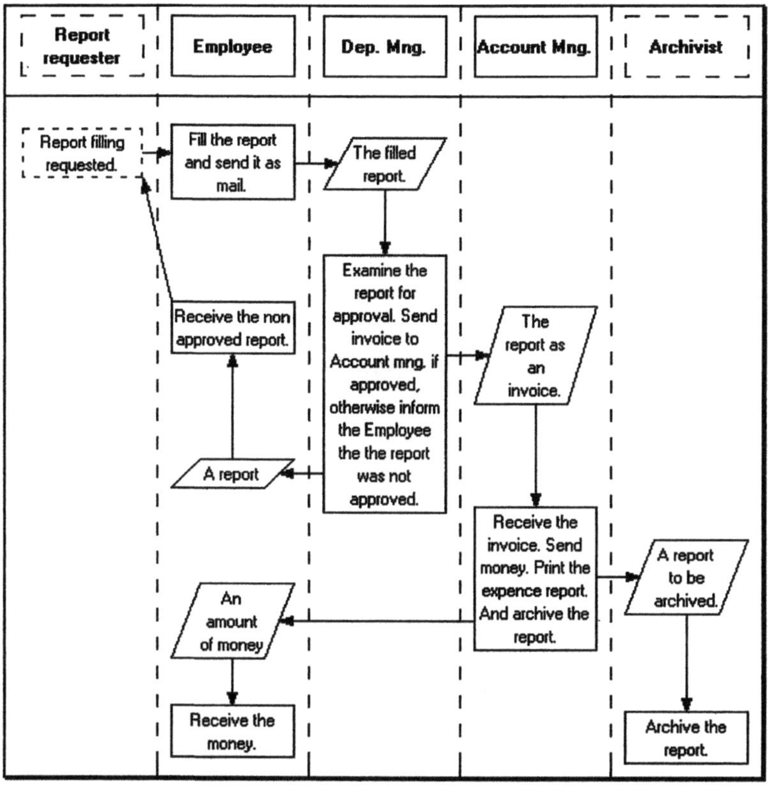

The actions in the process view also include condition descriptions. Explicitly one cannot show what is the yes or no branch of the flow. From the figure above it should be obvious what is a yes branch and what is no branch.

Figure 3-12 - The state view for the role Department manager

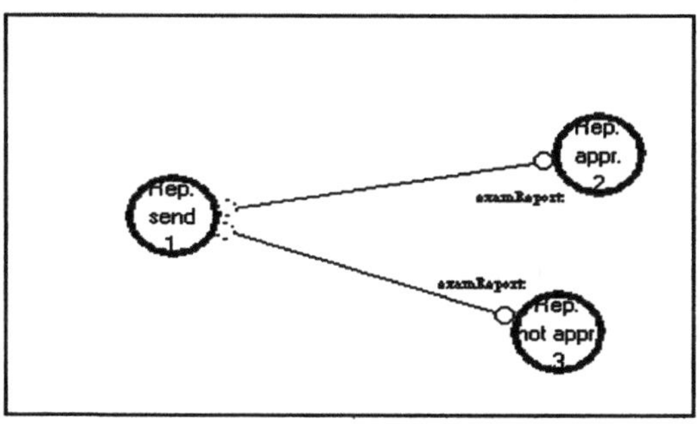

The Department manager role can either approve the expense report or disapprove the expense report. In both cases he or she will send the expense report to someone.

Figure 3-13 Action(s) of the Dept. Manager when approving the report (SDL)

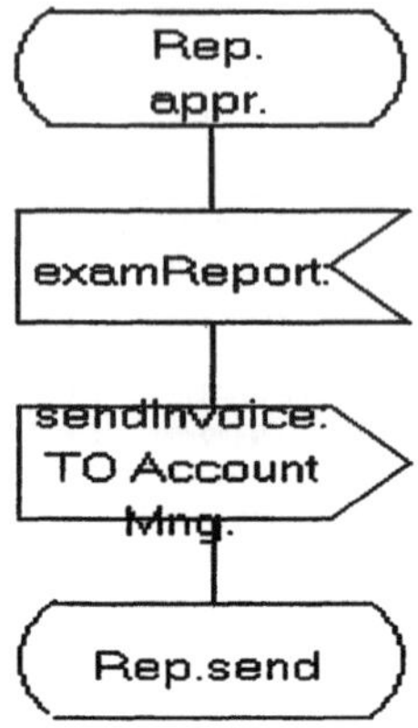

The figure above shows that the role sends the message (a sendMessage) *sendInvoice:* to the role **Account Manager** when going from state **Report approved** to state **Report sends**. Employee and the other roles also have state views and action descriptions in SDL, but we skipped them here for simplicity. The concepts are the same as illustrated for the Department Manager role. In the Orchestra workflow tool example there is some more information attached to the actions and conditions. In OORAM every element in model can have an explanation or text attached to itself. This text may contain information such as mandatory, etc. In the OORAM Method view, the same situation will be viewed as in the figure below.

Figure 3-14 -The Method View

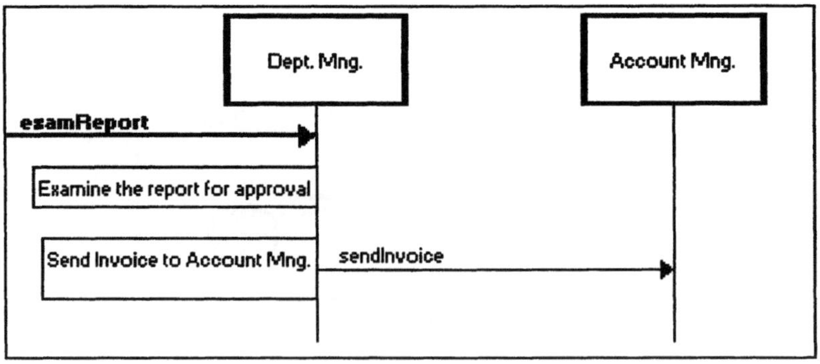

The table below shows the concept mapping between the two approaches.

Table 3-1 -Concept mapping between the basic elements

OORAM	Orchestra's workflow tool
Role model	Flow
Role	Role
Message	Stage
Interface	Transition
Method Block without sendMessage	Action
Method Block with sendMessage	Condition

What to model where

We can separate the workflow modeling problem into tree different areas:

- **The Business Processes**, where the high level business processes, the organizational roles etc. are described. These processes will be modeled in OORAM.
- **The Workflow Level**, where the actual workflows are described. The OORAM models from the Business Process layer may be detailed to specific workflows, and transferred to the Workflow Tool. If we start at the Workflow layer the workflows may also be modeled directly in the Workflow tool
- **The Workflow Support Level** where we describe the details of the workflow: Which templates to use, access rights to documents, etc. This information will be added in the Workflow Tool.

The Transfer level. The information stored in the OORAM models may be extracted by a set of general queries. The Workflow datamodel could have been loaded directly from OORAM by specialized queries, but to make the solution more general the transfer from OORAM to Workflow is done through a relational datamodel for the OORAM information.

The Datamodel level. From the datamodel with the OORAM information, transformation to different datamodels may be done through a set of SQL queries.

The Physical Database Level. In this specific solution, MS Access is used for the OORAM information and Oracle for the Workflow information.

3.2 Office and Workflow Platform

The functionality's provided by the office and organizational system provided by the Orchestra project have to be understood in the context of the integration with a base system, Elenix. In fact, Elenix Multimedia 3.0 is an office and organizational system that results partially from the integration of some of the Orchestra developments in the previous product[13].

Figure 3-15 - Elenix Multimedia environment and document archive

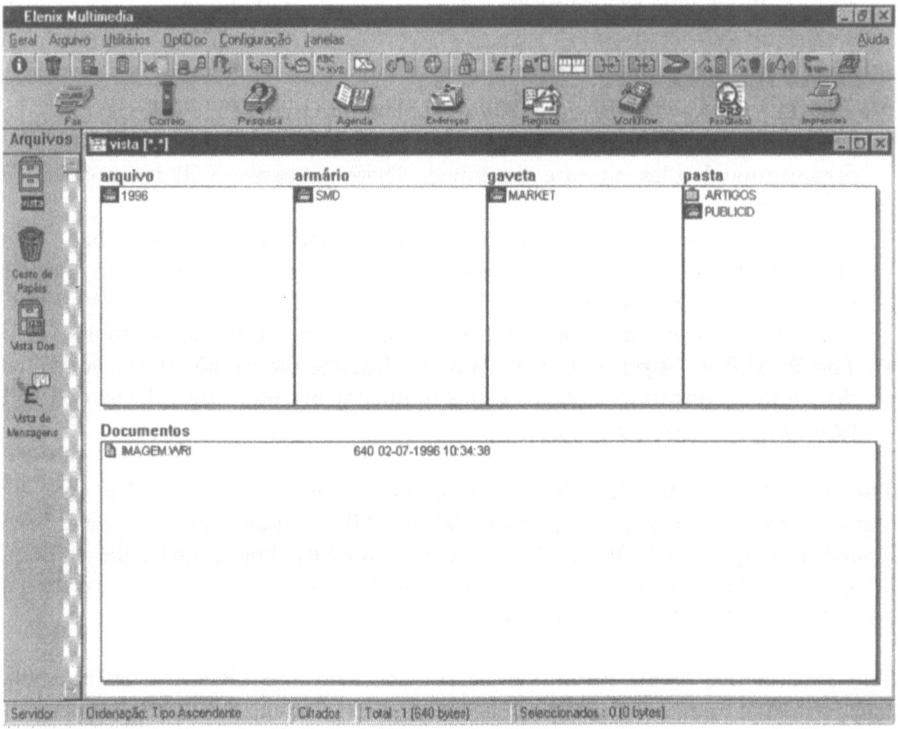

Elenix Multimedia is an integrated client/server office product for MS-Windows, Windows NT and UNIX, that offers a set of services to the organization. Some of these services are generic office automation tools which have been enhanced with Orchestra technology, like security, or mainframe access. Others are specific innovations, like the Workflow support, which is described in a dedicated subsection.

---

[13] Elenix Multimedia 3.0 was presented to the public in the Annual Elenix Users Group meeting, held in Lisbon, on June 96.

Examples of the previously existing generic office functionality, grouped in Orchestra under the expression User Environment, are:

- Local and Remote archiving of documents : Local archiving is performed on each client PC work site, Remote archiving is based on NFS (Network File System), and it allows the sharing of document archives residing on the server, among the PC work site.
- Electronic mail: used to interchange mail messages (with document attaching and audio annotations) among the Elenix users or to external sites. It allows parallel and serial messaging.
- Fax : It allows the sending and receiving of faxes from a PC work site.
- Document search and retrieval: It allows the indexing of documents (both on local and remote archives).
- Day Planner: It allows the scheduling of appointments, resource management, to do lists, and busy bars for fast scheduling.
- Registration of Correspondence: It allows the registration of the incoming and outcoming correspondence in the enterprise. It allows document routing through electronic mail.

A fundamental notion that has to be present in the analysis and evaluation of the efforts carried out in Orchestra, is the fact that commercial and marketing decisions have had a clear impact on the design and construction of the new functionality. To be more specific, SMD bases its strategy on the fact that the functionality is provided at a LOW COST per client installation. This implies that new functionality, like the workflow described below, while it may exist in commercial products, it does not exist at a cost that permits its integration without dramatic impact in the cost structure of the Elenix product. In several situations, licensing from third parties and integration is simply not feasible.

3.2.1 The Orchestra User Environment

The design and development of an enhanced user environment, evolving from the existing base system, Elenix, considered three components: (1) the evolution of the Archive system, dedicated to Document Management; (2) the design of a lightweight mechanism for document generation; and (3) the shell of the whole system. The design of this later component was considered premature until all the other set of services of Orchestra had been designed. Moreover, productized versions of Orchestra will not necessarily include all the technological elements described in this report.

3.2.1.1 Document Management in Orchestra - Archive14

The Orchestra Document Archive supports storage and manipulation of documents. It offer its own user interface and also a functional interface to other Orchestra modules.

The Document Archive was designed (based on previous generations) with the following **usability** requirements in mind: (1) ease of use; (2) document location transparency with respect to magnetic or optical media, local or remote filesystems; (3) document content transparency; (4) hierarchical structure; (5) a generic and commonly accepted set of operations.

Another set of functionality relates with the support for the **document life cycle**. These include:

- Document Profile - Document Archives directly based on operating system filesystem services do not support document profiling adequately. This functionality requires document database support. The profile information should contain searchable and tractable information such as : Author(M), Title (M), Subject (M), Keywords (M), Abstract (M), Creation date (A), Access Log (read, change) (A), User identification by access (A), Origin (moved from..., copied from..., document dragged from email message, etc.) (A), Previous names (A), Previous versions (see below) (A). Some of this data is filled automatically (A), while other may be filled manually (M).
- Dead Archive - Real world archives in organizations are required to support the "Dead Archive". This archive maintains deleted documents, folders and archives.The Orchestra Document Management system provides tools to manage this dead archive (activation and deactivation, house keeping).
- Version Control - The document version control maintains the incremental versions of documents,. Besides profile information, the version control system records some additional data : Version number (A), Version author (A), Date (A), Comments (M). Creation of new versions are explicitly done by the users.
- Integrity Control - Document Integrity control is a service provided by the Security Subsystem (see below). This functionality supports detection of file tampering by privileged users (such as system administrators), other than file owners.

The Document Management system is one of the intensive users of the **Security** services designed for Orchestra. These later will be described thoroughly in a following section. At this point, we highlight the set of services used to provide secure document management. These are:

---

[14] Based on Orchestra Deliverable D 2.1.1 - Specification of Archive, authored by Mário Romão, SMD

- Authentication of users as a prerequisite for document access and manipulation,
- Document access permissions, configurable on a per-operation basis,
- Encryption of documents,
- Location management.

3.2.1.2 Document Generation in Orchestra [15]

The Document Generation Module assists in the production of standardised documents (forms, text documents, etc.) required in any organizational setting[16]. The Document Generator has the following features:

- Produces documents according to a dynamic and organisation-specific set of rules. This implies: integration with other systems, to obtain the dynamic and organisational information to incorporate in the document generation rules, and ways to define the model documents for each organisation; generic document generation rules; ways to build new organisation-specific rules.
- Automatic and seamless integration with the Workflow and Global Information subsystems, increasing information consistency across the organisation.
- Interactive support for the production process (interactive form filling);
- Field value validation, in interactive document production.
- Automatic production (with no human intervention) of several instances of the same document type, with data being from other Orchestra components.
- Integration with other tools in the user-environment, a MS-Windows based environment, through standard MS-Windows communication techniques such as DDE (Dynamic Data Exchange) and OLE (Object Linking and Embedding).
- Documents are generic MS-Windows applications files.

Some security issues have been addressed in the Document Generation facilities.

- Access privileges by user and groups of users to Document Types: the system validates whether a user has privileges to generate a document of a given type.
- Access privileges by user to individual rules: the system validates whether user has privileges to trigger the application of a certain rule, in the context of the Document Type being used.

---

[15] Based on Deliverable D2.1.2 - Specification of Document Generator, by Mário Romão, SMD.

[16] As mentioned above, the document generation system of Orchestra was designed to be a lightweight and low cost system. Document Generation and Maintenance in large organisations is an area of work by itself, and heavy-duty systems using standardized tools (like SGML-Standard Generalized Markup Language), are obviously an important technology. This was however out of the scope of Orchestra.

- User authentication in interactive document production. For example, when in a workflow process, this allows each user the right to edit only the part of the document he/she is supposed to fill (e.g., certain fields).

3.2.2 Workflow

Workflow functionality plays a central role in the Orchestra project, up to the point where Orchestra has been coined several times as a "Workflow Project". There are several reasons for this relevance of the Workflow functionality:

- In the last couple of years, Workflow has emerged in the industrial arena as "the" new functionality to offer. This is the consequence of the evolution of traditional Office systems towards what has become known as Groupware systems. In a sense, the most obvious functionality of an environment like Orchestra is the workflow support. Also, for companies like SMD for example, the emerging and already available products (Lotus Notes family of products, Microsoft's Exchange expected evolution, existing specific Workflow products like Staffware, Flowmark) clearly identify competitive advantages and weaknesses.
- On the other hand, workflow technology is the most obvious need for organizations that deal with bureaucracy, i.e. paperwork, on a daily basis. While technologies for organizational modeling, or better communication, or support for decision making can be considered interesting and relevant in specific cases, managing routine (regulated) flows of work and information is a domain where technology impact is readily apparent and thus, a need is very easy to formulate.
- In the particular context of the European IT industry, Workflow seemed to be a *technological oyster*, where some pearls could be produced. Early experiences of ESPRIT projects like Prominand, products from Cap Gemini like Process Weaver, or Bull (Image Flow), the relevance of Staffware (from Staffware, a UK based company), supported (and they still do) the thought that workflow was still an area of product development that was not closed to European IT industry.

This is the context that was created for the design and development of a workflow system for Orchestra. As we describe below, the decisions made in this area where far from linear. The rationale for the workflow system design in Orchestra is presented below. The final functionality is, as this report is being written, being integrated in the SMD product, Elenix Multimedia 3.0. This product had its public presentation on June 26th, and is scheduled to be deployed in SMD clients (in Brazil) in September 1996. Given this level of finishing, the functionality will be described summarily described, and it can be fully observed through the SMD channels.

3.2.2.1 The Choice of a Workflow System Design for Orchestra

The initial approach to the design and development of a Orchestra Workflow component was based on the general notions concerning Workflow systems functionality and architecture. These led to statements like:

The workflow tool provides the ability to manage, monitor and control the execution of organizational procedures. The system allows the definition of information flows which are regulated by stages and conditions between stages. There are also notification procedures to warn a abnormal situations or to dispatch recovering tasks.

The design and development of the Workflow system was allocated to Novabase. The objective was to build a new workflow system, to be integrated with the remainder of the Orchestra components, namely what was the Elenix Multimedia functionality used as base technology and its foreseen evolution. The architecture was a client/server database, according to the taxonomies presented in "the Workflow White Paper" [Marshak94]. The efforts of the Workflow Management Coalition (WfMC) were not that evident in the beginning of the project but had subsequent influence, as will be understood in the architecture related chapter.

From the beginning, the project had to deal with the fact that Elenix Multimedia already included features like "circular lists" of mail messages, a very simple mechanism that suggested a way to another kind of workflow, the one which has been architecturally classified by Marshak as "mail-based". The coexistence of these two kinds of workflow support reinforces the need for integration.

The definition of the workflow functionality for Orchestra[17], the observation of the initial prototypes, the analysis and evaluation of competing products, and the result of the discussions and reviews, resulted in the following decision:

The workflow system of Orchestra would not be a standalone tool/system anymore, but rather a component with a much closer integration with the remaining Elenix components. The effort of Novabase was (re-)directed to the design and construction of an open and integratable Workflow Engine, upon which specific applications could be designed and implemented.

This decision reflects in fact the realization of the need for an open architecture for workflow systems, an approach that is being currently promoted by the WfMC (Workflow Management Coalition). As we will discuss later in the chapter devoted to the Orchestra architecture, this approach is very much in line with the WfMC proposals. From now on, in this chapter, the details of the Workflow engine will be forgotten since it has no direct impact in the Orchestra workflow functionality.

---

[17] Deliverable D2.2.1-Functional Description of Workflow Tool, authored by Filipe Carlos, Novabase

3.2.2.2 The Workflow Functionality in Orchestra

The workflow functionality provided in Orchestra is integrated and already available in the specific product of SMD, Elenix Multimedia 3.0. As mentioned above, the workflow functionality is provided by a set of client applications (client in the sense of Elenix, i.e. running on a user's PC), that interact seamlessly with a server component (the Workflow Engine) running in the Elenix Multimedia 3.0 server. The client applications, the ones that provide user functionality are the Flow drawing application, the Form design application, and the client Workflow application.

The use of the workflow system requires the understanding of a set of concepts users and workflow programmers. The following table summarizes these concepts.

Table 3-2 Basic Concepts of Orchestra (Elenix 3.0) Workflow[18]

Concept	Meaning
Flow	Defines process types
Process	The instance of a flow
Groups	Sets of users. Defined to designate work groups or users with common organizational profiles (secretaries, programmers, directors).
Group Head	The head of a group
Stage	A process is usually divided in stages. A stage encapsulates part of the work to be executed in a process
Stage Performer	The performer of a stage is the user, or group of users that is responsible for executing the work assigned to that stage.
Task	An action included in a stage. Tasks can be compulsory or optional. All the compulsory tasks within a stage must terminate for the stage to terminate
Condition	A condition that determines the next stage of a process.
Document	A file associated with the process. Files are associated to the flow (global files for all the processes of that type), process (instance files), or task.
Form	A form is an active document It is a view on the data stored in a database
Access Rights	These are the user default access rights to the processes of a given flow. Access Rights can be changed as the process executes.
Manager	The privileged class of user.
Accept Stage	Declaration of a user with responsibility for executing all

[18] See relation with WMC proposals, standards, etc...
http://www.aiai.ed.ac.uk/wfmc

	the tasks of a stage
Delegate Stage	Once a stage is accepted, it can be delegated to another user
Delegate with Validation	Delegate and later validate the execution performed by the other user
Current Stage	Stage or stages which are pending acceptance by a user. A process may have several current stages, when a flow defines parallel processing
Suspend stage	Change the status of a stage to suspended (from current).
Delete Proc	Stop the execution of a process and mark it as terminated. Processes are not deleted for a historical record is required.
Suspended Proc	A process is suspended when all its current stages are
Terminated Proc	A process is terminated when all its final stages are terminated
Pending Proc	A process is pending when it is not terminated
Automatic Numbering	The Workflow system allows the automatic numbering

The above mentioned applications, Flow Drawing, Form Design, and the Client Workflow, are targeted for different kind of users. The first two are to be used by workflow programmers, people in the organization that capture, define and program the flows. The later is the client application for the everyday user.

Figure 3-16 - Elenix Workflow Client -Interface for a User/Administrator

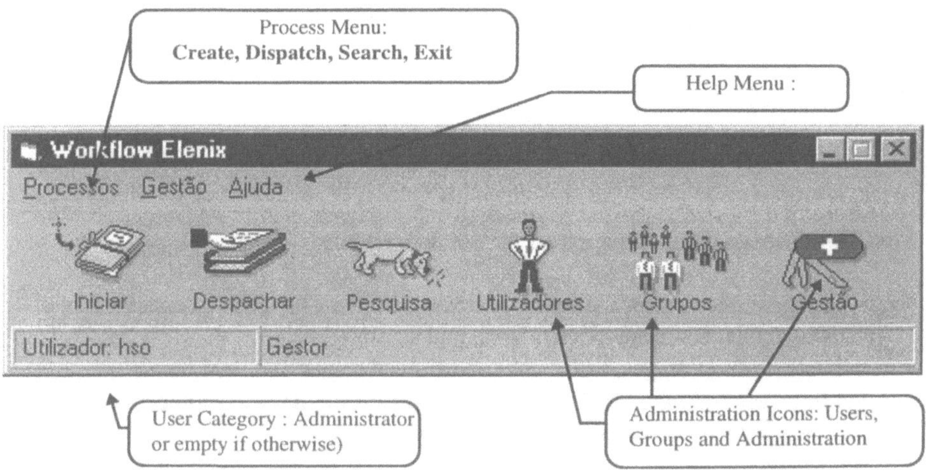

The Workflow Client Application. This application is the interface to the creation, dispatching, and follow-up of processes, as well as to some services

related with administration (process and flow management, users management, and so on). The figure below shows the main interface to these functionality[19].

The Forms Design Tool. his tool supports the drawing of the forms that are associated with a given flow. The tool allows to design the form layout, as well as the links between the form fields and the tables where the real data presented by the form exist in a database. These are the tables that were created in a database, simultaneously with the creation of the flow. The links between the tables in the database and the form fields are created through a supplied API (Application Programming Interface). The form design tool can be implemented with a variety of existing tools, depending on their existence at the customer location (Word 6 and macros, Excel and macros, Delrina FormFlow and macros, Microsoft Electronic Forms, VisualBasic).

Figure 3-17 Main Screen of Flow Design Tool

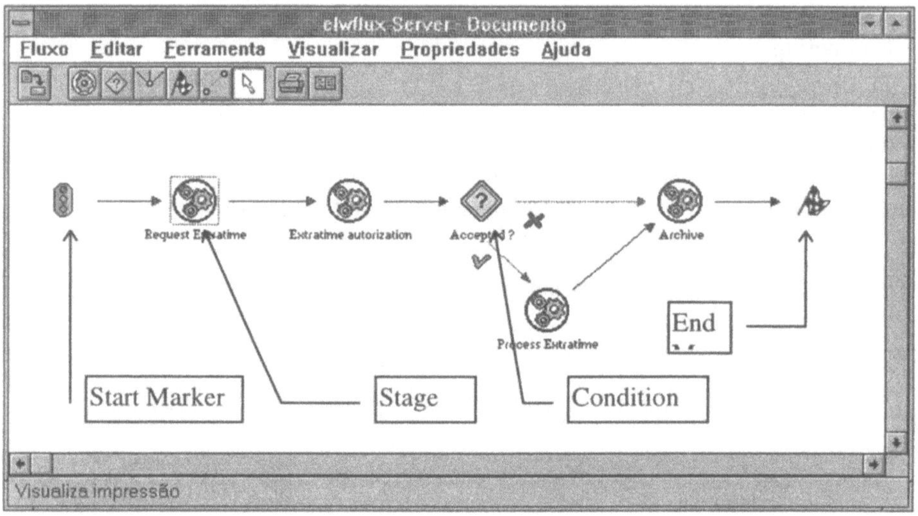

The Flow Design Tool. his application is composed of:

- a graphical flow editor including representations of the above concepts like arrows, icons, zooming mechanisms, and so on.
- the definition of stages, tasks and conditions through dialogue boxes
- the interface to build and manage the content of the database tables associated with variables to be used as fields in the above forms.

---

[19] Quick Translation by order of appearance (from left to right, top to down) : Processos = Processes, Gestão = Management, Ajuda = Help, Iniciar = Start, Despachar = Dispatch, Pesquisa = Search, Utilizadores = Users, Grupos = Groups, Gestão = Management, Utilizador = User, Gestor = Manager.

An overview of the tool follows (see Fig.3-10 and following):

- To create the flow, the user must first create the flow "layout" on the screen. Then, by selecting objects on the screen, the user defines their contents of each object (for stages, the contents means defining tasks, alarms, etc; for conditions, it means defining the condition itself, the variables involved, etc.)
- By using the option "Dados Gerais do Fluxo" (Flow Generic Information) of the menu "Propriedades" (Properties), the user can define the name and code of the flow, the deadline, etc. The screen used to define this is presented in Figure 3-11.
- The following screens are used to define the flow variables (variable name, variable type - text, integer, Boolean, decimal point number or signature - and variable default value (see Figure 3-19)
- The next screen (Figure 3-20) is used to associate or dissociate documents to a flow, through Drag&Drop from the Elenix Archive. The documents associated to a flow can be plain documents or forms. A form is a view over the variables in the database; through the form the user can read and write values in the variables, if he/she has access to perform these operations to a certain variable.
- This is the screen (Figure 3-21) the users get after selecting a stage object. From this screen the user can define the name and code of the stage, it's responsible group (role), it's tasks and alarms.

Figure 3-18. Flow Properties definition - Flow General Data

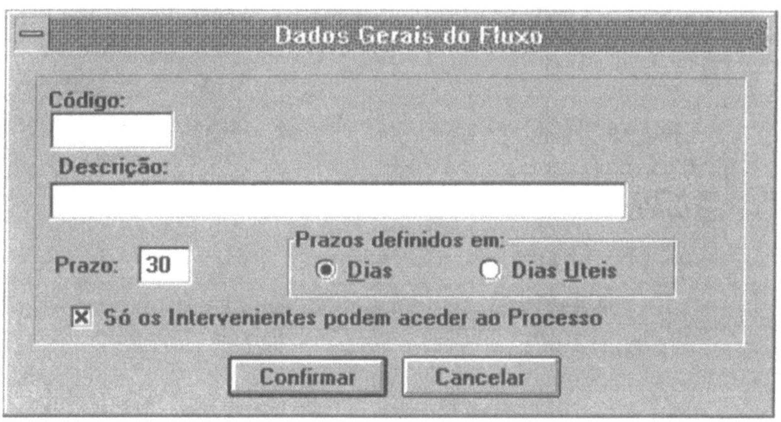

Figure 3-19. Definition of Variables in the Flows

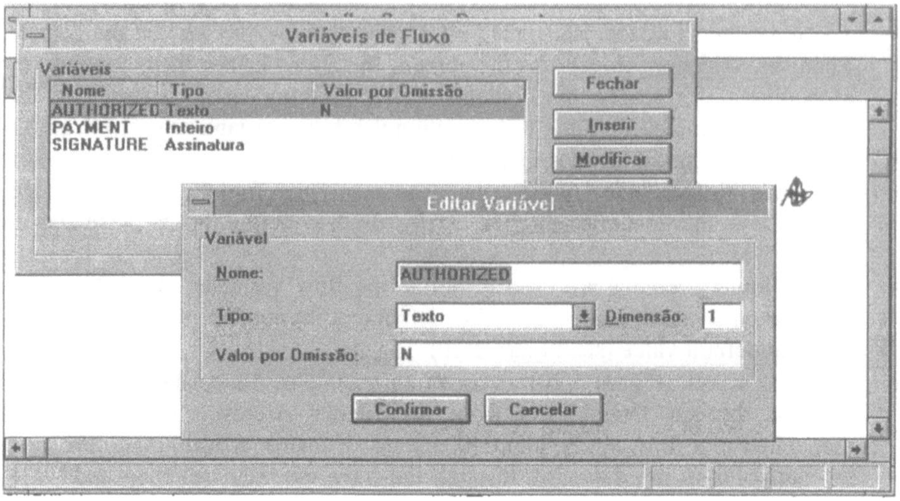

Figure 3-20. Association of Documents to the Flows

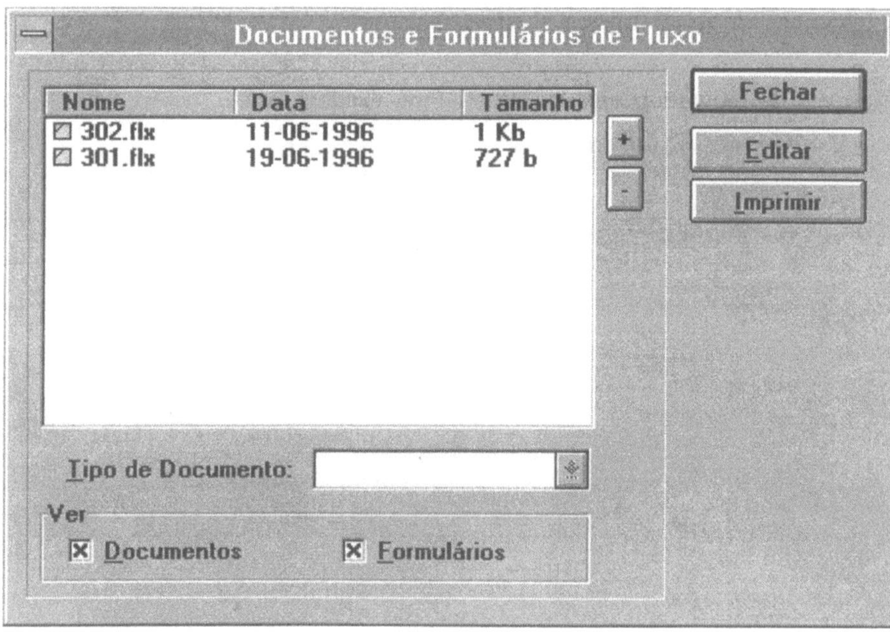

Figure 3-21. Selection of a Stage in a Flow

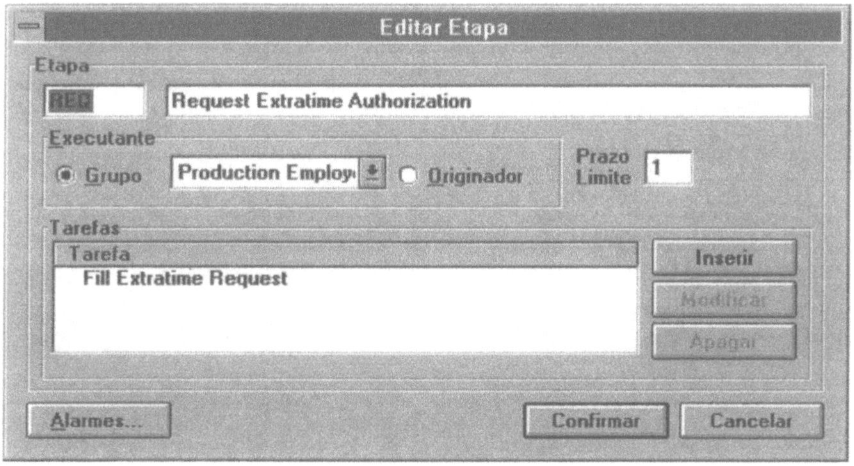

The next screen appears when the user clicks the Inserir (Insert) or Modificar (Modify) button next to the tasks list of the stages screen (previous picture). Here it is possible to define the task, if it is mandatory or not, and what action should be performed in the task. The action to perform in a task can be: Manual (it's the users responsibility to do something), start a command, start a form, send a mail or send a fax. The action is selected in the combobox "Operações Automáticas" (Automatic Actions), and the lower part of the screen chances according to the selection. This and the next two pictures depict the screens for defining the "Start Command", "Start Form" and "Send Mail" actions.

Figure 3-22. Task definition in the Workflow (1)

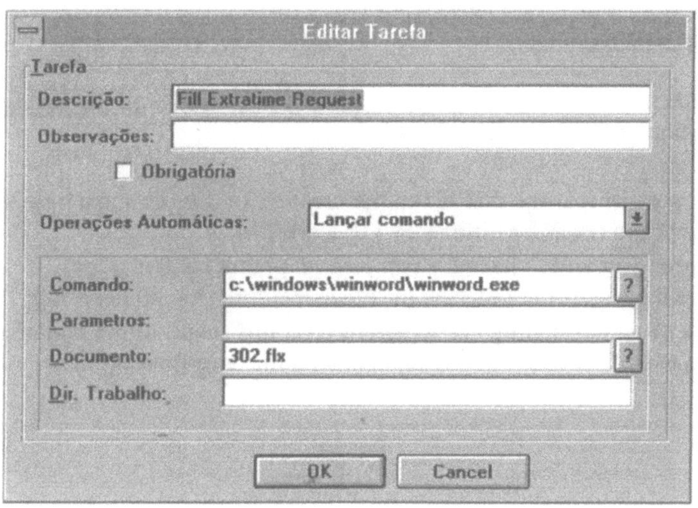

Figure 3-23 - Task definition in the Workflow (2)

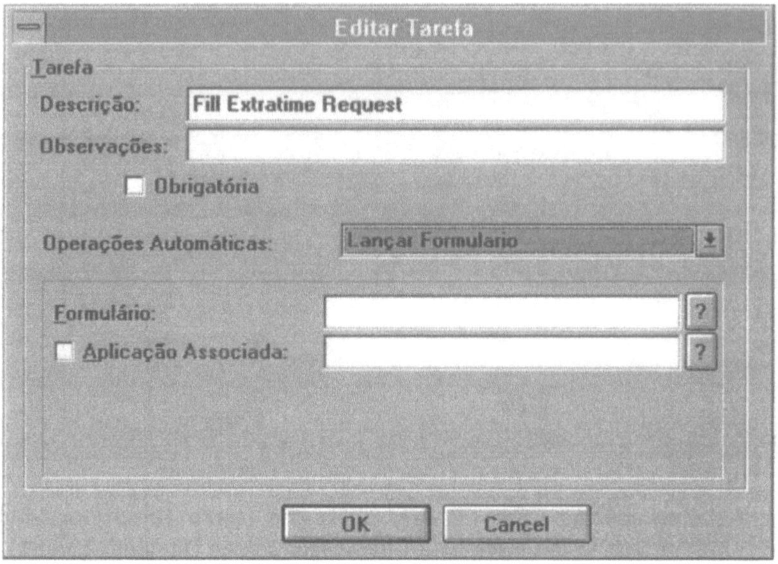

3.2.2.3 A Comment on the Workflow Definition Functionality

The objective of the Orchestra project in terms of Workflow modeling was in fact reflected in the approach presented in section 3.1.2 above. The goal can be summarized in the following statements:

- do not reinvent modeling functionality,
- profit from high level concepts for reusability,
- extend existing tools.

This is what has been proposed, and technically achieved, with the use, integration, and extension of OORAM from Taskon.

There are several reasons that led to the creation of a basic modeling set of tools for the Orchestra (Elenix Multimedia 3.0) workflow:

- The need and will to launch a commercial product at this stage,
- the need for assuring low cost for Elenix Multimedia 3.0 licensing,
- a lack of understanding and experience (at this stage) of the real effectiveness of the use of OORAM in conjunction with the workflow engine.

- a lack of evaluation of the impact of using a high level modeling tool in workflow modeling for the generic client organizations (needs for expertise and training)
- At the moment when the Orchestra results are coming to an end, this fundamental notion of separation of Workflow Modeling and Enactment, which is being pursued by the Workflow Management Coalition and is now reflected on the proposals mentioned above (the Process Definition Language), is now conceptually proved. The follow-up efforts are dependent on the will of the industrial partners involved in Orchestra to match their efforts. Specifically, a clear direction is the evolution of the Taskon OORAM Tool to support PDL generation at some level, and the evolution of the Novabase/SMD workflow engine to be compatible with PDL. If these two steps are followed, the loop will close.

3.2.3 Security in Orchestra[20]

As mentioned in chapter 2, a set of fundamental relations among people and groups in any organizational setting are the authority relations. These are typically materialized in role assignments, authorizations, capabilities that are delegated, permissions and prohibitions, rights and obligations. The enactment of these flows in a technological platform is very much related with support for security, authentication and privacy. This the reason of the effort made in Orchestra in the security domain.

The Orchestra Security subsystem provides a set of cryptography-based mechanisms and services to achieve adequate and flexible levels of security. The design of the security mechanisms and services takes into consideration the execution environment and specific needs of the several components of the ORCHESTRA distributed system.

3.2.3.1 Assumptions Concerning the Orchestra Environment

For the design of the ORCHESTRA security functionality, the environment is assumed to have the following characteristics:

- **Unsecured local network.** Nodes of the distributed environment are connected by an unsecured local network, allowing wire taps, replay, or tampering individual messages. Such attacks raise privacy, authenticity and integrity problems.
- **Secure external connections.** The local network is connected to the outside world through secure gateways that acting as fire-walls.

[20] Based on Orchestra deliverable D 2.3.1, authored by André Zuquete, INESC

- **Secure central machine.** All the servers implementing the services provided by the ORCHESTRA system run on trusted machines. These servers are the only entities of the system that are allowed to interact with information systems located in external information servers (for example, mainframes).
- **Unsecured client terminals.** Users interact with the ORCHESTRA system through personal computers (MS Windows). Applications running in these machines are open to intentional and non-intentional virus attacks. Two type of attacks can be expected: software modification and data steal. The first one raises the need of software authentication and on-demand download from a secure central node. The second is much harder to prevent due the lack of separate and protected address spaces.

3.2.3.2 Orchestra : a Secure Environment

To address the above problems, the functionality provided by the Security subsystem was designed to include the following features: authentication of users, secure communications, secure data storage, and key management.

Authentication of Users. The authentication of users is a basic requisite to perform any kind of access control or role assignment. Access control or role assignment policies are defined and enforced by several components of ORCHESTRA (Archive, Workflow, Document Generator, etc.). The security subsystem cooperates with all these components by providing the means to correctly identify the users responsible for the requests issued to them. The public information on users, that can be used in such identification, is stored in a directory service.

Users must authenticate themselves when they log in the system by means of a name and a pass-phrase. Users login as specific persons, not as members of groups or responsible for roles. The authentication process follows and, on success, all the necessary credentials of the users are kept to allow applications to further authenticate the user vis-à-vis any ORCHESTRA service (like in Kerberos-based systems). Credentials have an expiration time.

Each user is allowed to access a subset of the ORCHESTRA services. Such subset is managed by the security subsystem and is embedded in the user's credentials. This information can be used to load, from the central secure machine, fresh, certified and authorized client modules to access central servers. Such download and certification reduces the danger of voluntary or involuntary corruption of the client's code.

The two kinds of attacks that can occur in a client machine can expose pass-phrases and credentials managed by the system. While credentials can be designed in order to minimize the danger of such exposure, the disclosure of pass-phrases represents a significant threat to the system trust. The solution to this problem is an open issue and was not solved in the current design and implementation.

Secure Communications. To achieve secure communications in peer-to-peer or client-server interactions, the following functionality was designed and provided:

- **Authentication** - users or servers running interacting applications should authenticate to each other. All exchanged messages can be authenticated by including ciphered (e.g. using a secret session key) or signed (e.g. using DSS) well-known data. The particular cryptographic algorithms to be used depends on the nature of the interaction and on the underlying communication mechanisms used to support it. Per-message authentication allows non-repudiation with proof of origin, i.e. a message receiver can unambiguously prove its origin and this cannot be forged. The encryption of well-known data may be an important input for a known-plaintext cryptanalyst. Thus, the knowledge of that data from outside the context of the communicating peers should be reduced to a reasonable minimum.
- **Integrity** - any message should arrive to the receiver as it was sent (data integrity) and the reception of message replays should be detected and ignored[21] (protocol integrity). The integration of ciphered (or signed) Message Integrity Checks (MICs) and timestamps/sequence numbers in each message allows a receiver to check the integrity of each message and the coherence of a sequence of messages.
- **Privacy** - messages circulating in the network should be ciphered so that wire taps could not reveal their correct contents. The cipher key can be defined or agreed upon the connection is established (either solely by the interacting peers or using the services of a trusted third-party), or defined per each exchanged message. A mixed solution can also be considered. Using only a new random key per each exchanged message implies its distribution, along with the message, to the receiver (e.g. using public key techniques).

These AIP properties (Authentication, Integrity and Privacy) are introduced in different levels of the communication stack. In ORCHESTRA, they are introduced in three different ways: (i) ad-hoc, in messages exchanged using directly transport protocol APIs (sockets/winsock or NetBIOS), (ii) implicitly, as features of a secure RPC package, or (iii) in mail messages according to standard or widely accepted formats (e.g. PEM or PGP).

Secure Data Storage. The AIP properties also improve the security of stored data. Authentication techniques can be used to sign individual updates of archives (files, databases, etc.), thus committing users to the new archive contents. Integrity protection prevents data from being modified in an undetectable manner. This is achieved as a side effect of the authentication previously referred if one signs a

---

[21]Or, more correctly, reported to system administrators.

MIC of the updated data instead of the data itself. Finally, it is possible to cipher sensible documents when access control mechanisms are not enough to disallow unwanted disclosure (e.g. by the system administrators). However, the management of the cipher keys to crypt archives is a responsibility of the Archive, and not of the security subsytem.

Key Management. Users digital signatures require the use of asymmetric cryptographic algorithms and pairs of secret/public keys: the secret one to generate a signature and the public one to check its validity. This way, users are bound to specific and unique key pairs used to manage their own signatures. Assecret keys can be lost, disclosed or broken, users should be able to get, whenever necessary, new secret/public key pairs. However, old signatures spread all over the system (including in archive backups) must continue to be usable, and that is no longer possible with new public keys. Thus, the security system keeps a history of all public keys used and still in use. This history allows to correctly check old signatures and detect signatures generated with stolen or obsolete secret keys.

3.2.4 Global Information System

The fundamental reason behind the somewhat pompous name "Global Information System" is the attempt to bridge the gap between traditional large scale, mainframe-based information servers, used and managed by the support staff of our previous organizational model, and the universe of personal computing or groupware computing, used by the anonymous office worker of an organization. The approach that underlies the provision of this integration functionality (which is believed to be of a growing relevance as the buzzwords legacy systems become more widespread), was to incorporate existing and proven technology, in our case from Software AG, and produce a proof of concept with potential for further exploitation after the project.

Two main areas of concern where defined in Orchestra. First, a solution for system interconnection had to be found. Second, a systematic approach to data access and manipulation.

3.2.4.1 Connectivity in the Orchestra Environment22

The trend assumed in Orchestra states that two usually separate functions, centralized data processing and departmental end-user computing, must be combined to yield what is called enterprise computing.

[22] Based on Orchestra deliverable D.2.4.1 - Connectivity Systems and Interfaces, authored by José Antonio Frias, Software AG

Central corporate resources must be available to more and more knowledge workers. As a result, the island solutions that have been created in different departments must be integrated into enterprise-wide computing. This increases the necessity of dealing with heterogeneous, distributed systems. Requirements for flexibility and extensibility of software applications lead to a services-oriented architecture with clear separation between User, Business, and Data Management Services, together with flexible boundaries with respect to where are the clients and where are the servers.

Connectivity Objectives in Orchestra. The connectivity goals in Orchestra are focused on the integration of connectivity systems between ORCHESTRA based clients and servers in heterogeneous systems and machines. The requirements of the Global Information system match the main yardsticks (mentioned in Chapter 2). Moreover, the Global Information system is responsible for providing these features to the rest of modules. These are autonomy, conformance to standards (DCE, CORBA, X/Open), generality (LAN's and WAN's over SNA, DECnet, X.25, TCP/IP), interoperability, openness and performance.

Approach to Global Connectivity. Software AG's ENTIRE middleware was the underlying technology for client-server computing in ORCHESTRA distributed environment. The ENTIRE BROKER set of functions is the central building block for constructing distributed applications and cooperative processing. It provides connectionless and conversational communication interfaces between applications running on conventional mainframes, UNIX platforms, PC workstations and other platforms. The main characteristics are:

- **Portability:** Applications using this programming interface for program-to-program communication and client-server communication need to be easily portable to different hardware, operating system and network system platforms.
- **Language interoperability:** Programs written in third-generation languages must communicate with programs written in NATURAL (Software AG's fourth Generation Language, for access to relational and legacy databases) and viceversa.
- **Common programming interface:** The programming interface will support various program-to-program and client-server communication models (conversational, request/reply, asynchronous communication).
- **Multi-transport protocol communication:** The ENTIRE middleware supports heterogeneous transport protocols (see table 1.1 below) and is used to integrate different network architectures (LAN, WAN, enterprise networks).
- **Legacy application integration:** The ENTIRE middleware technology is ideally suited for the integrating legacy applications into distributed open systems.
- **Network traffic reduction:** Applications based on distributed or remote data access often cause non-affordable network traffic, due to the fact that data

selection can only occur after it has been moved from the DB server to the client machine.

The ENTIRE BROKER accepts requests from multiple clients and matches these with the corresponding services offered by servers in the environment. Together with the transport layer ENTIRE NET-WORK, the BROKER provides a ready-made transport mechanism for service requests and responses. ENTIRE NET-WORK is the connectivity backbone, that shields clients and servers from network characteristics such as different protocols and network topologies. All client and server programs operate transparently, as if they were linked locally. Table 1.1 summarizes the operating system and protocol compatibility of NET-WORK.

Table 3-3. ENTIRE NET-WORK availability

	TCP/IP	SNA	SPX	Netbios	DECnet	other
OS/2	✓	✓	✓	✓	✓	
Windows	✓	✓	✓	✓	✓	
Windows NT	✓	✓	✓	✓	✓	
Macintosh	✓		✓		✓	
OpenMVS	✓	✓			✓	X.25
UNIX	✓	✓				OSI
OS/400		✓				
WANG VS	✓	✓				WSN
MVS	✓	✓			✓	CTC
VSE		✓				
CMS		✓				
GCS	✓	✓			✓	
BS2000	✓					DCAM

3.2.4.2 Global Access and Manipulation23

One of the main guidelines that define the evolution of data management strategies and technologies in large organizations is the distributed approach. Previously isolated departmental databases, are now becoming accessible to every member of

[23] Based on Orchestra deliverable D.2.4.2 - Specification of Data Access and Manipulation , authored by José Antonio Frias, Software AG

the company. On the other hand, large centralized corporate databases are sometimes being partitioned into local work subsets, synchronized with a master copy. The distribution of Data Management Services (defined as complementary to User Services and Business Services) across the organization resources must be flexible and capable of being adapted to each situation in order to make optimum use of system resources, such as computing power, storage capacity, network capacity, etc..

The requirements for flexibility usually lead to hard heterogeneity problems in software and hardware components: departmental machines and systems are usually different from those used in enterprise computing environments; existing Data Base Management Systems (DBMS's) and programming languages are often difficult (if not impossible) to connect. Moreover, there are cases in which legacy data bases (based on non-relational data base models, like Hierarchical or Codasyl) must be maintained for a number of years.

An approach to solve these problems has been the definition of standards. The Relational database model is the most widely used model in current DBMS's (so called Relational Data Base Management Systems or RDBMS's). The generalization of RDBMS's led to the ANSI standard data definition and manipulation language called the "Structured Query Language" or SQL, a standard that has its own caveats[24].

Objectives for Data Access and Manipulation. The Data Access and Manipulation functionality of ORCHESTRA addresses the definition of the data base connectivity interface for distributed and heterogeneous data bases.

A significant requirement for the Data Access and Manipulation is, as above with Connectivity issues, the conformance to standards : ANSI SQL will be the primarily adopted standard for data base access and manipulation. Also ODBC for Windows systems and specific SQL extension for DB2 are supported. Additionally, a Flexible SQL facility will accept any other special SQL syntax extension, that will be passed to the corresponding SQL Server for dynamic (run-time) parsing and execution. Relational databases are therefore widely supported. However, the technology adopted by the Global Information system also allows other common DBMS's and Data Manipulation Languages.

Approach to Global Data Access and Functionality. Software AG's NATURAL and ENTIRE middleware are the enabling technologies for data access in the ORCHESTRA distributed environment (see figure below).

---

[24] Discussed in Orchestra D 2.4.2 - Specification of Data Access and Manipulation, J.A.Frias, SAG

NATURAL[25] is the Software AG's fourth generation language, designed for the development and maintenance of database-oriented applications. NATURAL is acknowledged by the EC as strategic technological asset (Document IX/E-6(86) S10-1043-12, Chapter 4.5). ENTIRE is an integrated solution for Client/Server computing: ENTIRE ACCESS is the centerpiece of an unified interface for access to heterogeneous relational database management systems from NATURAL programs. ENTIRE BROKER provides a communication interface and connectivity services between client and server modules. ENTIRE NET-WORK was mentioned in the previous section on Connectivity.

Figure 3-24. NATURAL and ENTIRE technologies for distributed and heterogeneous data access

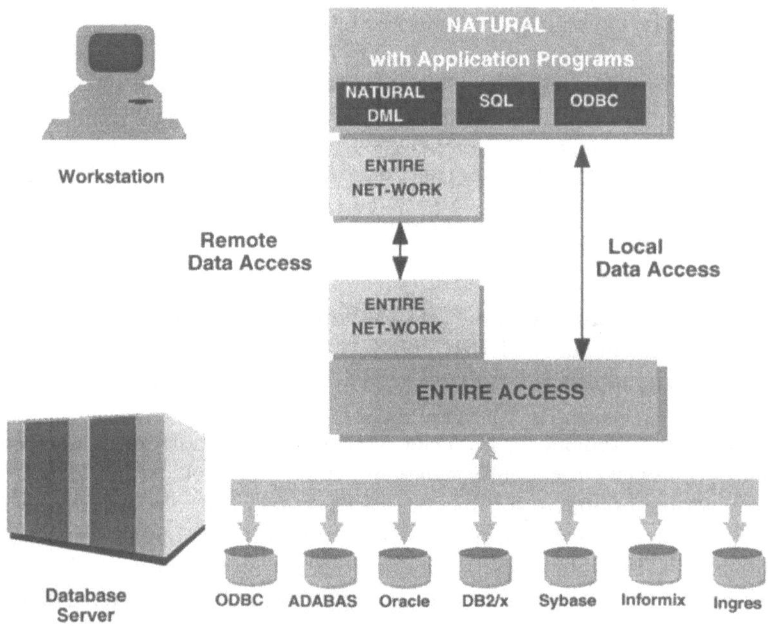

Based on these technologies, the Functionality of the Data Access and Manipulation Support results in a set of functions, available to ORCHESTRA components and services that provide uniforms access to a universe of information servers and databases. These functions, to give the reader some insight, include Basic data access functions to either relational or Non-relational databases, like

[25] For further information on NATURAL and ENTIRE, see the above mentioned deliverable or contact Software AG.

Creation of records, Single and Multiple Record Selection, Record deletion, Record Modification, Transaction Management, Extended SQL functionality, ADABAS-specific functionality, DB2-specific functionality.

3.2.4.3 A Fast Query Mechanism

The availability of a powerful integration platform for connectivity and data access led to the design and development of what was called, a Fast Query system. The main features of such a system, once again justified by the will to produce stronger integration between end-user computing and corporate systems, are:

- Support for conceptual reference to available data, instead of using technical names of files and fields. This allows the logical abstraction from the physical database structure (for example, coupled files), and would be performed via intelligent interpretation of the Data Dictionary.
- User interface based on dynamic menus, for a flexible and easy definition of the type of access, the logical condition criteria, the display layout, etc.
- Transparent access to distributed databases and heterogeneous DBMS's. The user does not need to know where the data are located, neither which DBMS's are holding them.

The Objectives of the Fast Query Tool.

- High-level logical abstraction from the physical database structure: the user does not need to know technical names of files and fields. Files are conceptually considered as entities, and fields as attributes.
- Minimum (if not null) training time for end-users, by means of a very flexible, user-friendly and easy-to-use interface. Based on dynamic menus, this interface will perform an intelligent assistance for the selection of entities and attributes, definition of the kind of access, specification of logical condition criteria, selection of the attributes to be displayed, etc.
- Use of NATURAL programming and database access facilities, as well as the ENTIRE middleware infrastructure, for transparent access to distributed databases and heterogeneous DBMS's.
- Integration with existing applications via NATURAL, that is, a specified query could result in a NATURAL program that makes use of existing procedures (standard calculations, already developed and tested routines, etc.).
- On-line generation and execution of optimized NATURAL programs, meeting the requirements that have been expressed in the dynamic menu interface.

The Fast Query as seen from the End User. Fast Query is a tool which facilitates the flexible definition of database access queries. Queries defined using Fast Query can answer to two kind of questions: on the one hand, questions about the number of occurrences of an entity which satisfy a condition; and, on the other, the values of a set of fields for the instances of an entity which meet a condition. These query conditions can not only refer to the value of the fields/attributes of an entity, but to the relationships between entities. Fast Query provides a very intuitive end-user interface (in English, Spanish and Portuguese) for the flexible definition of this kind of queries. After the query definition, an optimized NATURAL program, which interrogates the database for the records satisfying the query requirements, is on-line generated and executed. This program is stored on a directory and can be later edited, modified, and/or executed.

The final user operating mode is based on an easy interaction through dynamic menus. These menus are automatically created depending on the specific server in which is going to run, and the DBMS's which will be accessed. A typical session covers the following stages:

- User identification. In order to prevent unauthorized access to confidential data, the user must be authenticated.
- Execution profile. There are several execution parameters which can be customized by the end-users. These are:
  - Interaction language: The end-user interface is available on three different languages, English, Portuguese and Spanish.
    Database which the user want to access to: The conceptual model of this database has been previously defined and loaded into the Fast Query tool by a system administrator.
  - Storage directory: Users can specify the directory where the generated programs will be stored.
  - Output device and text format: The result of the query can be displayed at the screen, be directly sent to a printer, or be downloaded into a PC file. The end-user can select one of these devices for his/her query outputs. Also, different formats are possible for the output texts, a table screen template, ASCII plain text, ORCHESTRA document generator readable, etc.
- Identification of entities for query formulation. The first step on the query definition is the selection of the entities which the user wants to obtain field values from. The list of database entities is presented on the screen as a select box menu. The conceptual names of entities are displayed, along with meaning and purpose, to facilitate the selection to users not familiar with data structure and technical names.
- Determination of the type of query. Two different kind of query can be defined by using the Fast Query utility. It is possible to define queries which determine the number or retrieve the values for entity fields of entity instances satisfying a condition criteria.
- Selection of the desired attributes: The attributes which value in the entity instances satisfying the query will be reported, are now selected. After the entity selection, a menu with the list of attributes of the previously identified entity is dynamically generated. This menu is presented as a list box. Also, the conceptual attribute descriptions are displayed instead of the internal names.

Figure 3-25. Fast Query Interface (1)

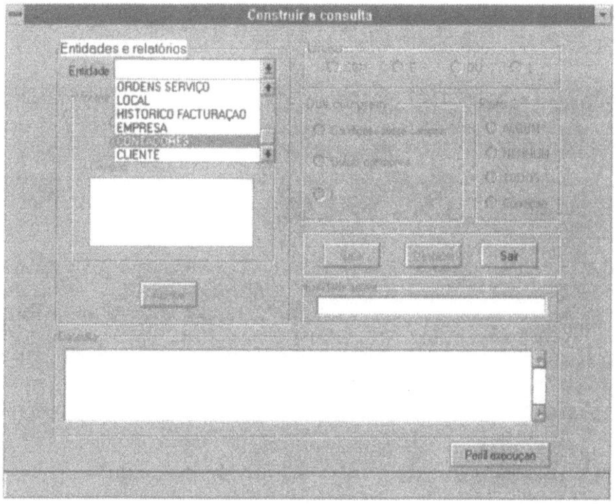

Figure 3-26. Fast Query Interface (2)

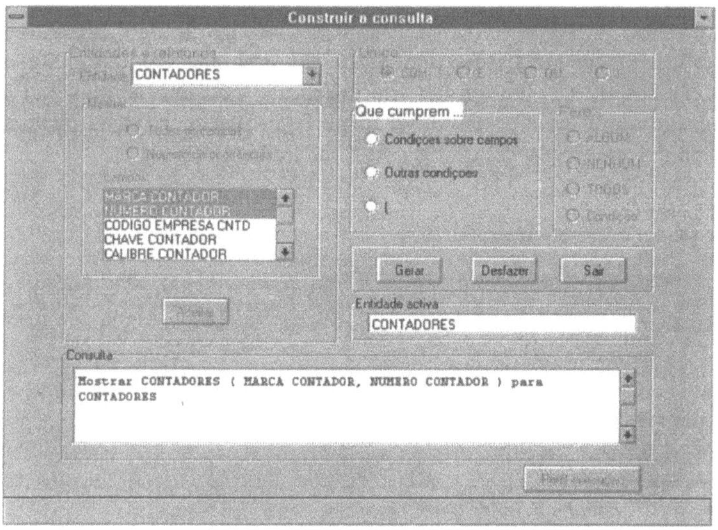

- Definition of the conditions of the query: The user is allowed to define, in a declarative way, the conditions query result must meet. This conditions can refer the entity attributes or to relations between different entities. A different window is available for the determination of a condition based on the attributes of the active entity. There are a set of operators (AND, OR, NOT, opening and closing brackets) for the construction of complex conditions.

Figure 3-27. Fast Query Interface (3)

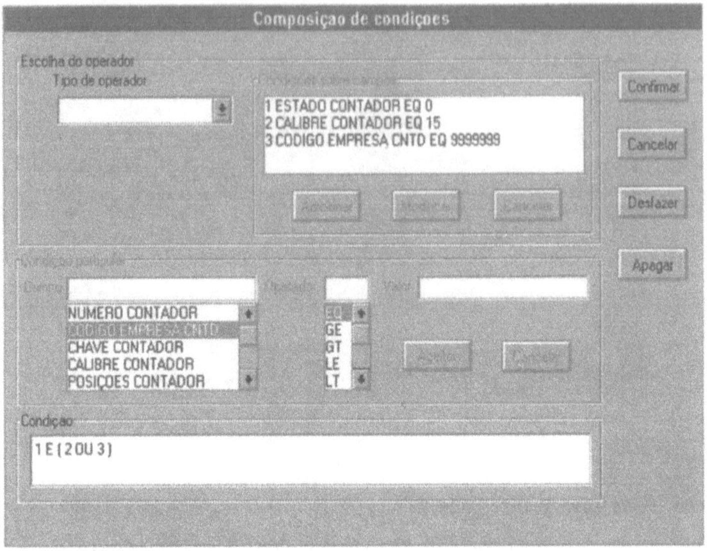

- Generation of the query program: Once the end-user has completely detailed the query conditions, the application interprets the requirements and generates a program which will be executed to perform the query. The program which has been automatically created is saved for future retrieval.

Figure 3-28. Fast Query Interface (4)

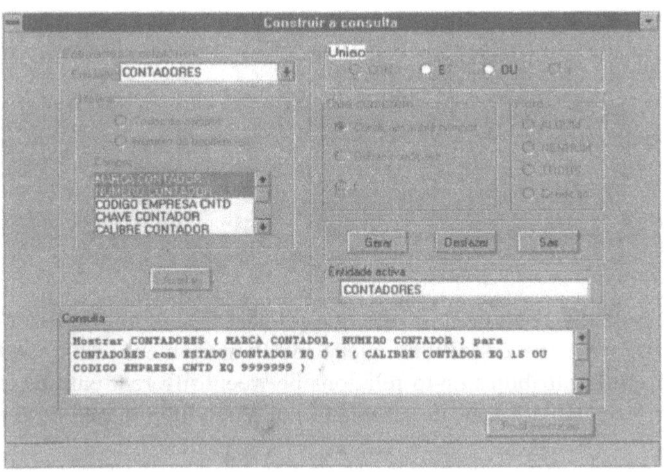

- Final report: As final execution, the results of the query are displayed at the screen or unloaded into the printer or a PC file according to the parameter specified during the definition of the execution profile. Depending on this profile, the result of the query can be downloaded PC file with a format readable for the ORCHESTRA Document Generator module. This property facilitates the creation of reports.
- Use of the programs: NATURAL programs generated for the query to the database information are saved. Subsequent these programs can be edited, modified and/or executed. This allows the periodical execution of standard queries, and the specification of similar queries just modifying the program of a previous one.

3.3 Communication

Communication in Orchestra means technological support for enhancement of the communciation processes within an organizational framework. More specifically, the goal is to design and develop technology that improves personal communication, as well as group communication.

The simplest form or communication is the one that occurs between members of an organisation, supported traditionally (if tradition of computer-supported work already exists in organisations) by electronic mail. In this scope, the goal of Orchestra was more technical than conceptual. In fact, a small effort was dedicated to the standardization of electronic mail or, more generically, messaging, through integration of standard interfaces (MAPI) in the base platform (Elenix). The initial prospects (stated in the Proposal and Technical Annex) have considered enhancing informal communication with audio- and videoconferencing. However, having these technologies been considered somewhat orthogonal to the remainder of the project technologies[26], and due to the lack of immediate interest from the pilot organisations, this aspect was abandoned.

The augmentation of group communication, in the sense of work constellations (as presented in the Rationale of Chapter 2), led to the proposal of a functionality called contextual communication. This functionality, which was not completely

[26] The enhancement of "closed" interactive multimedia technologies, like videoconferencing, with organizational awareness should be relevant to the generic Orchestra objectives. Limitations on resources are however obvious in any project. In any case, work on media indexing, media parsing content analysis can have impact on the integration of multimedia supported communication processes with complementary organizational information or automation components.

clear at the beginning of the project, showed, with the evolution of the design and implementation, to have high potential for changing and improving communication in organisations. Going back to the project's acronym, the issue addressed is how to include some organizational awareness in the communication processes that occurr in organisations, be they internal or external. The section that follows describing the Contextual Communication functionality provided in Orchestra clarifies how this problem has been tackled.

3.3.1 Enhanced Messaging [27]

Many organisations are looking to their electronic messaging system to take on the role of a central communications backbone, used not just for electronic-mail (e-mail) messages, but to integrate all types of information. With the emergence of powerful enterprise-wide workgroup applications for scheduling, forms routing, order processing, project management, and more, the need for such a communications backbone has been growing.

Microsoft created the messaging application program interface (MAPI) standard to help ensure complete system independence for messaging applications. MAPI does this by taking its design from the Windows printing model. Just as Windows allows applications to print to a variety of sources (using a print spooler and independent printer drivers), MAPI allows messaging applications to work easily with a variety of messaging services.

3.3.1.1 Standard Messaging for Orchestra

MAPI is part of the Microsoft® Windows open services architecture (WOSA), a design created to hide programming complexities from both users and application developers while providing seamless access across a variety of systems. As the messaging component of WOSA, MAPI is the result of an effort among Microsoft and more than a hundred independent software vendors (ISVs), messaging system providers, corporate developers, and consultants from around the world. MAPI is an open API; it can support virtually any client messaging-enabled application, including advanced workgroup solutions, on any messaging system.

The Design for the Orchestra Messaging system. Using the MAPI architecture and concepts as a starting point, we proceeded with the requirements for an open messaging subsystem in Orchestra.These include:

- a MAPI messaging system provider (driver) for the Windows operating system
- a messaging system server for UNIX and for Windows NT

[27] Based on Orchestra Deliverable D.3.1.1, authored by Nuno Duarte, INESC

The availability of Microsoft MAPI transport providers (drivers) for MS-Mail messaging system (in Windows/Windows NT operating systems), allowed the immediate support of the Orchestra messaging subsystem in this environment.

In the case where UNIX operating system happens to be the server, the SMTP electronic mail industry standard is the most plausible choice to be used. This leaves us with the task of developing a Windows MAPI transport provider for the UNIX messaging system (SMTP/POP3) that supports virtually every UNIX mail system and seamlessly integrates security in all messages exchanged through this subsystem.

The transport provider performs the following tasks: authenticate the client to the mailbox in the Mail server; convert MAPI messages and attachment to messages contents according to the RFC822 and MIME standards and vice-versa; send and receive messages to and from the UNIX Mail server using the TCP/IP protocol offered by the Windows sockets network API as the transport protocol, SMTP as the application level protocol for sending messages, and POP3 as the application level protocol for receiving messages form the UNIX Mail server; support PEM standards in order to sign sent messages and validate other users signatures in received messages; secure messages contents against disclosure or modification.

Integrating Services at the Desktop MAPI makes it possible to integrate multiple, diverse messaging services at the desktop. This means that an e-mail, fax, voice mail, and bulletin-board service could all be reached through a single client application acting as a master communications window. Rather than have a separate in box for each messaging system, users can enjoy the simplicity of a single universal in box to consolidate all of the various message types.The user simply installs the drivers for the appropriate services, just like printer drivers for different printers.

Messaging-Aware Applications MAPI allows basic messaging capabilities to be easily integrated into virtually any desktop application. Using the Simple MAPI calls, developers can add message capabilities to their applications' own user interfaces. A word-processing program could be enhanced to include a Send Message option next to the print selection. Such an option would send the document as a mail message to a recipient. Applications are called messaging-aware when they do not depend upon messaging for their functions. That is, the basic messaging capabilities provide an additional value to the regular features of that application.

Messaging-Enabled Applications Unlike messaging-aware applications, messaging-enabled applications require some type of messaging capability in order to function. One example is a scheduling application in which users can view the schedules of their coworkers and send meeting requests to the coworkers' calendars. Another example is a forms-routing application that sends an expense report to a series of recipients and records their approval or disapproval.

Messaging-Based Workgroup Applications The most advanced type of messaging application is the workgroup application, which requires full access to all of the back-end messaging services, including the message-store, address-book or directory, and transport functions. These applications include e-mail clients, workflow automation programs, and bulletin board services. For example, a workflow application might allow a user to inspect a message stored in a certain project folder to see if the appropriate workers have signed off on their tasks. This application could also include a sophisticated search-and-store feature that retrieves relevant files from a bulletin board system and stores them in the folders of certain recipients.

3.3.2 Contextual Communication Services28

Organisations receive lots of documents daily: Letters, packages, faxes, electronic mails, written in different languages. All this information must be distributed to its destination. The full address of the receiver is usually indicated in the document. So these should be distributed properly. However, life is not that easy. Sometimes, problems could occur, like:

- No address is indicate, in which case it is necessary to search for the right addressee based on the document content..
- The receiver is unknown. This case is solved in a similar way as above.
- The address is difficult to understand. Here, the names of the people in the organisation should be compared with the one of the addressee. Later, if no distribution is possible, the document is handled as a document without address.
- There are several people in the organisation matching with the address. Some information about the department or the subject of the content has to be be analyzed in order to determine the adequate receiver.
- The receiver is a department instead of a person. The content is analyzed to determine the person in the department who is interested in that information.
- The address indicates a person of a department and the person changed to another department. The content is analyzed to determine whether the subject of a document is personal or relates to the department. In the first case, it is

[28] Based on Orchestra Deliverables D.3.2.1 - Specification of Formalisation and Classification and D 3.2.2 - Specification of Distribution Tools, authored by José António Frias, Software AG. These reports provide extensive information concerning all the submodules described in this section. The description made in this report is a summary of the functionality provided. For detailed explanation, please refer to the mentioned Deliverables.

sent to the addressee person, in the second, the new person in the addressed department who is working on that subject will be determined.
- The receiver has left the organisation. The solution is similar to the previous one.

Moreover, many documents arrive to a newsgroup and the users spend too much time reading useless information. Profile specification helps in minimizing this waste. While much of this functionality exists in available products and public domain technology, it is a by-product of the Orchestra Contextual Communication design, which benefits from the global concern for organizational awareness.

The Contextual Information system helps to solve the above problems. Its objective is to receive information from an internal department or external organisation, formalize it, classify it, and, finally, distribute it to the right person or groups of people.

The Contextual Communication functionality of is divided in two different modules:
- The Formalisation and Classification Machine normalizes and classifies received documents. The information structure and semantics of the text content are analyzed.
- Distribution Machine. This module determines the distribution mechanisms based on the results of Formalisation and Classification.

3.3.2.1 Formalisation and Classification of Messages

As mentioned above, the Contextual Information Subsystem is divided on two different modules: Formalisation and Classification Machine and Distribution Machine. The Formalisation and Classification module (referred next as F&C) determines the information receiver. This is done through document analysis and, if necessary, through semantic text processing.

The input documents are supposed to be in electronic format. Several types of documents are supported: electronic mail; News (bulletin boards); Faxes (complemented with OCR); Closed documents or Packages (complemented with manual introduction of data); other documents like (telex, press news, billing, technical papers, magazines, etc.)[29]. Each one of these types of documents is processed differently, due to their different internal structures. A detailed description of the processing approach is presented in the mentioned Deliverables.

The processes addressed in the F&C module are organized in the steps depicted in the figure 5, and described below.

---

[29] These last formats were not considered for prototyping purposes in the scope of the Orchestra project.

Figure 3-29. Formalisation and Classification steps

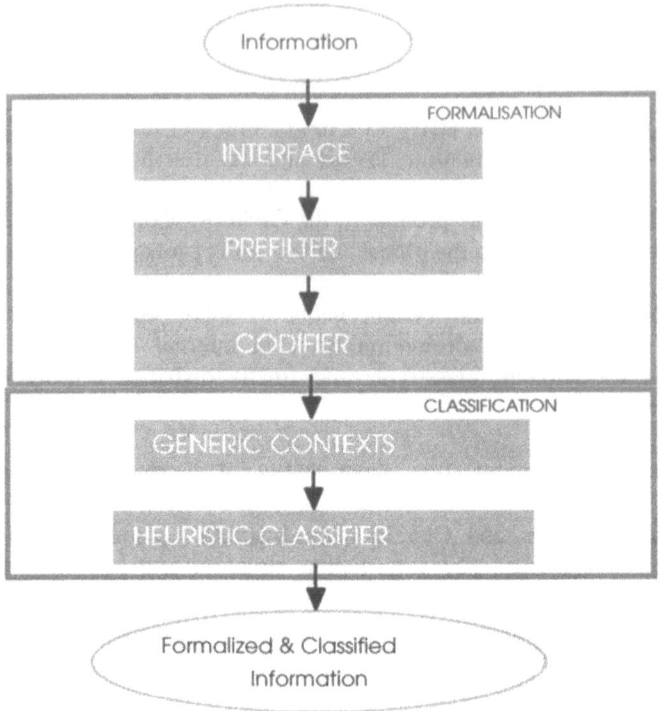

1. **Interface:** The first step is the acceptance of the unit of information. The interface provides a flexible data input path, accessed from other ORCHESTRA modules, as well as external programs.
2. **Prefilter:** This module analyzes structure of a document and determine the strings or blocks of text containing significant topics; for instance, kind of document, name of sender(s) / receiver(s), date of emission, number of pages, addresses, title, abstract, body text, etc.
3. **Codifier:** This process matches the obtained strings or blocks of text against corporate information in order to identify relevant topics referenced in the document. For example, text string in "sender" slot will be translated to the corresponding person code or company code. Misspellings are corrected, initials and abbreviations expanded and ambiguities solved. When any of the related persons does not appear in the directory of the organisation, the codification module will try to structure names and addresses. Other topics considered will be department names, jobs, locations, references to other documents, etc.

4. **Generic Contexts Module:** Initially, a shallow analyzer checks a set of filtering criteria and decides if the structured information obtained so far is sufficient for distribution purposes. In this case, next stage (semantic knowledge extraction) could be bypassed. If necessary, the Generic Context module is responsible for the extraction of semantic knowledge contained in the document. This process is directly based on document contents as well as on additional data structures representing basic knowledge about keywords, synonyms and phrases, the organisation itself and status of internal activities (information provided by Workflow subsystem). This approach allows the proper interpretation of semantic knowledge in its correct context.
5. **Heuristic Classifier:** This module carries out the final classification of the element of information in order to determine what element of the organisation should receive it. While the generic contexts module establishes the general frame to which the current element of information belongs, and will try to be mostly organisation independent, the heuristic classifier is organisation-dependent knowledge.

The Formalisation includes points 1 to 3, while Classification deals with points 4 and 5. Distribution is addressed in another module of the Contextual Communication Subsystem. However, both subsystems are closely related.

Some aspects related with free text recognition provide an understanding of the scope of the F&C module.

- Multilingual environment: the prototype recognizes English texts and conventions. However, the system design will allow the inclusion of additional languages; such as Spanish and Portuguese.
- The basic structure of a dictionary is included, supporting synonyms, aliases and related concepts.
- Recognition of multiple international conventions: date & time formats, numeric symbols, currency, measurements, punctuation, special characters (ñ, ç,...), etc.
- International Calendar Management: weekdays names, months, seasons, year periods, some important national and local holidays, etc.
- Recognition of corporate information: employees, departments, jobs (interface with the Directory in the Communication Subsystem), projects, tasks, responsibilities (Workflow Subsystem).
- Background knowledge with partial updating facilities: countries, main cities, etc.
- Maintenance of an internal log for processed documents, in order to allow further control system performance, recognize cross references and learning capabilities.

3.3.2.2 Distribution of Messages

The process performed by the Distribution Machine (DM) depends on the results of the Formalisation and Classification module. The Receiver Entities that will be considered by the Distribution Machine are generated by a specialized module, based on information provided by the Workflow subsystem and existing Directory services.

The distribution decision process is based on a knowledge-based system. Users specify their rules in a simple declarative mode. A rule-based system is used to implement the modules that interpret the distribution rules, check the constraints and take the decisions. Document delivery is coordinated with the email facilities. Optionally, the fax server could be considered for final distribution purposes.

The DM includes the following elements: the Distribution Routines, the Central Administration Service, the User Administration Service and the Internal Data.

Distribution Routines These procedures perform the access to the Receiver Entities, interpretation and execution of the distribution rules and final delivery. The distribution process is organized in steps shown in the figure below.

- Expansion of addressees : This submodule takes the receiver(s) suggested by the F&C Machine and will expand the groups to the person in charge of receiving the documents. For instance, the secretary is usually responsible of the documents that arrives for her/his department.
- Application of distribution criteria : This submodule produces a new list of receivers applying the distribution criteria. Some of this criteria are based on company guidelines, other are user defined. These rules consider user preferences, carbon copies to responsible persons, and so on.
- Delivery of the document or notification : Performs the distribution to a list of persons to whom it should distribute the document, and sends to each one a message through the email system. The message contains the document or a notification that a document has arrived for her/him.
- Central Administration service. Some domain-dependent information is considered in the distribution process. The organizational information from directory services and Workflow Subsystem must be reflected on the internal structures (Receiver Entities). Some different level of organizational guidelines for the document distribution could be defined by an administration service.
- User Administration Service. The distribution process is also guided by a user profile and her/his preferences. These represent the areas the user is interested in, her/his absence periods, and other user-dependent parameters. This module provides a user interface for configuration purposes.

Figure 3-30. The Distribution Routines

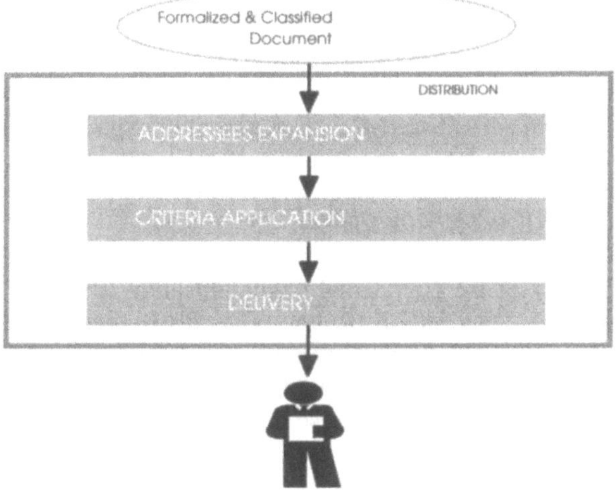

- Internal Data. The DM uses some information to support the distribution. Some of this data is common to the F&C module, for instance, the dictionary; and other ones are specific to this process, such as, the Receiver Entities, distribution rules, user profiles and preferences.

Some additional features of the Distribution Machine are outlined below.

- Explanations facility: The person who receives a document from the Distribution Machine, is always able to ask for the reasons that led to such decision (document addressed to him, selected by a specific subject, redirected to the alternate user, rule or set of rules fired, etc.). This will help the user to adjust her/his own profile.
- Log maintenance: Every distributed document is referenced in a log file, allowing off-line processing such as tracing, accounting, feedback for administration, etc.
- Retrieval functions: Some important retrieval facilities are provided. For instance, after an absence period, a user is able to ask for every received document that was addressed to him/her and redirected to an alternate user. Also, some statistical process could be performed (total number of bulletin board documents found per subject, and others).
- Intelligent rule maintenance: The central and user rule administration is able to detect and correct situations such as rule redundancy, cycles, inconsistency between rules, etc.

The DM is divided in three modules, as mentioned above and depicted in the figure below: Central Administration, User Administration, and Distribution

Routines. The details of each represented block are available in the corresponding Deliverable report.

Administration tools. There are some administration tools which can be used by a system administrator to centrally define and maintain the organizational context, local geographical and administrative data, organization-specific dictionaries, etc. All this information characterizes the behavior of the Contextual Engine, since it defines the "context" of the organization. The Central Administration Tools allow to adapt these data to the changing context.

Another functionality of the Contextual Communication System is the definition and maintenance of Distribution Rules. The distribution rules contain the information to determine to whom the document will be delivered. They allow the receiver entities to declare the documents they are interested on, who else should receive the documents they receive, and so on.

The distribution rules can make references of distinct points; for example:

- A rule could ask about the current status of a person, e.g. sick or on vacation.
- It will be possible to mention the subject the received document is about.
- Different kinds of receiver entities are considered: individuals, departments, projects, informal groups, groups related with products or services, and so on.
- The references to persons can be defined directly to the individual or to the job.
- The specification that the whole document is required or that a small notification about the document will be necessary depending or not on the document size.
- The delivery medium will be able to be selected (email and fax considered).

The Distribution Rules Maintenance tool allows the definition of complex conditions over the document characteristics (sender or addressee properties, size, data and time, semantic contents, geographic origin, etc.), and the selection of the requires actions (distribute copies or notifications, define alternate addressees on absent periods, etc.).

The Distribution Rules Maintenance tool can be run after login in the ORCHESTRA environment. It allows users to view all their distribution rules grouped by type -personal, group and organizational rules. Any rule is identified by its validity data, creation date and a brief textual description. The possible actions are: create a new rule, modify a rule and delete an obsolete rule.

Figure 3-31. Rule Viewer window

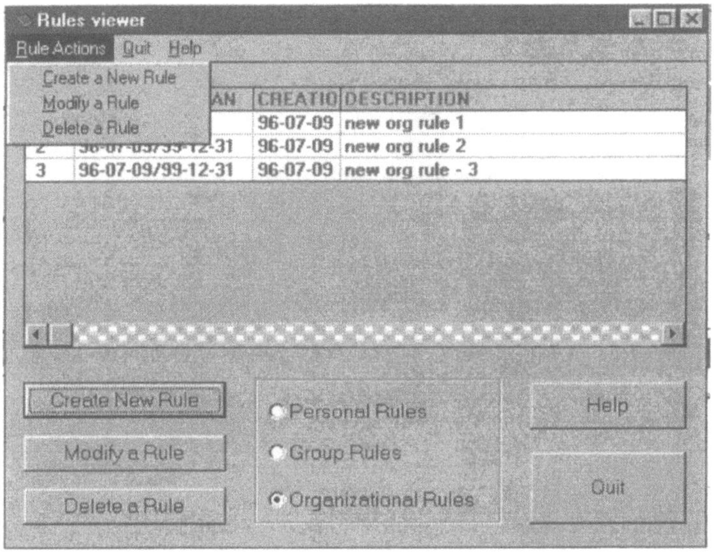

The Rule Maintenance window allows to design new rules of all types. Each rules have three parts: a general information, an antecedent part and a consequent part. The general information fields show: the type of the rule and its identifier (fixed automatically), the validation and expiration date and a brief textual description of the rule. The antecedent section contains conditions on receiver and document characteristics. The conditions are connected by means of the logical operators and can be organized hierarchically using parenthesis. The Consequent section fixes new receivers and new formats of distribution for all messages corresponding to the antecedent conditions. In order to avoid the user mistakes in writing rule, only the correct buttons are active, that is if you have not opened a parenthesis, you can not use the button corresponding to a closing parenthesis. Both antecedent and consequent component buttons will provide users the guidelines to write new line in the antecedent and consequent parts, making complete the line step by step.

The antecedent can contain conditions on possible senders/receivers attributes and on document features. For each sender/receiver, the end-user can choose between conditions on various attributes: name, role in the organization, working group (dealing with a project, a product and so on), organization, fax / phone / E-mail, and, in case of a condition on receiver attributes, current working status (working, ill, no longer working at the organization, absent, on vacation,...).

Figure 3-32 Rule Maintenance window

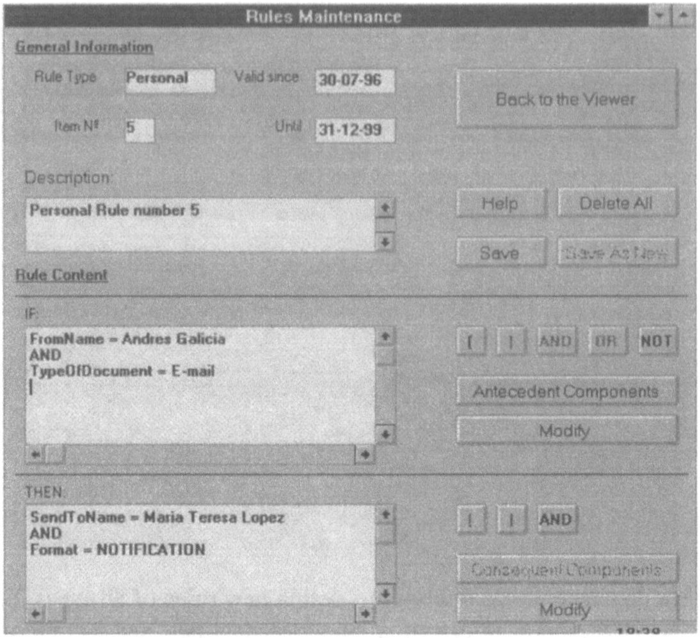

Figure 3-33 Rule Programming Interface

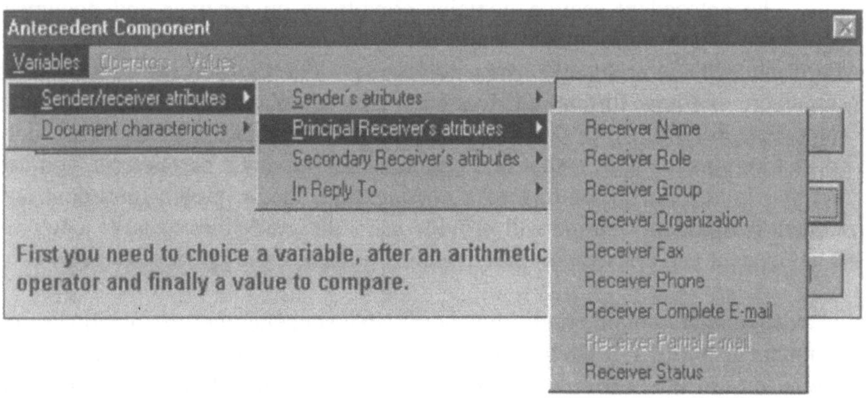

Conditions on document features are all that may filter the documents: its type (mainly fax and E-mail), its volume, its subject, its geographic origin, its main language and some semantic information extracted during the document processing (so-called Semantic Categories), which is a kind of general subject for the document (as business, technologies management,...). Also, the user could define if the rule can be applied to confidential and urgent documents or not.

Figure 3-34 - Rule Programming Interface

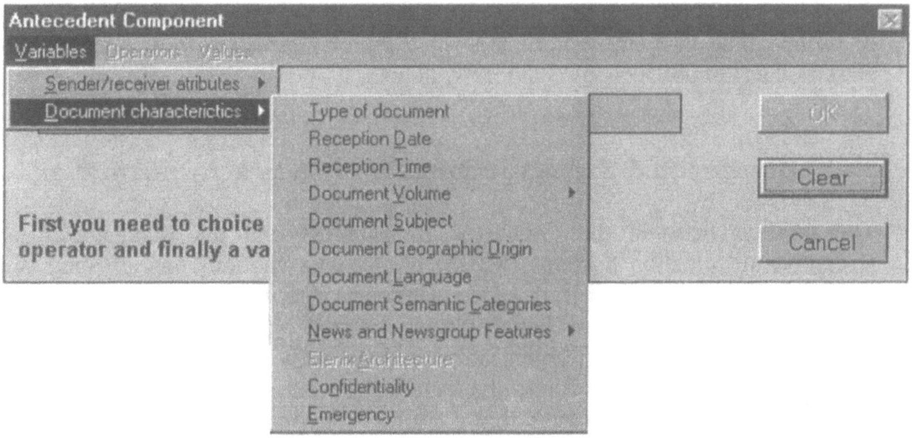

There are two ways to determine a value for each condition. The end-user can enter free text or use ORCHESTRA internal data. It is recommended to use the second way to improve the reliability of the rule. ORCHESTRA data covers a large range of organizational information. For example, all people of the organization people is registered in the ORCHESTRA receiver entities, with their role, working group, address, phone / fax and e-mail. Geographic places are covered too. To access this information, Distribution Rule Maintenance Tool has a graphical interface, which allows to navigate through ORCHESTRA database and select relevant data with the mouse.

3.4 Decision and Group Interaction

A final set of issues and corresponding technological designs that was included in Orchestra relates with decision and negotiation processes. These processes (or flows) correspond to the large group of ad-hoc decision processes that have been included in the organizational perspective early in the report. The question to answer has been, how to provide support for these flows in the Orchestra environment.

A major assumption underlying the design of the functionality to be provided was some degree of separation between what was called quantitative decision support, and qualitative negotation support. The former usually takes the form of Management and Executive Information Systems which allow quantitative reasoning and simulation that help in the decision processes of either individuals or groups. The later are materialized in a set of interactive tools that are often classified as Group Decision Support Systems.

3.4.1 Management & Executive Information Systems in Orchestra30

The relation between the Orchestra environment and the Management and Executive Information Systems (MEIS) has been a cautious one. In fact, some previous experience in projects and consultancy activities on the part of several members of the consortium, led to the generalized opinion that the choice of a particular EIS by any given organisation, and specially by large organisations, is a complex process, not only due to the technical decisions involved but also due to the particular class of end-users that a MEIS is supposed to have, i.e. very often top management. In this context, it would make no sense to direct the Orchestra environment to a specific MEIS. This is why the notion of MEIS plug came up. On the other hand, it was realized that the linkage between a MEIS and the workflow environment would have potential for creating added value in the domain of decision support.

A thorough review work has been performed in the initial stages of the Orchestra project and an available report[31] describes what is put into the term MEISs (Management and Executive Information Systems) and EIS (Executive Information Systems). Summarizing the information included in that report, we can state that the main objectives of Executive Information Systems are:

- Provide meaningful information to top executives, middle management and knowledge workers in a company or organisation, focusing on the following dimensions: time, quality, resources, deliverables, products and productivity.
- Control the management indicators and their evolution to watch over critical strategic factors needed to attain the organisation objectives.
- Detect deviations and tendencies, make statistical analysis, simulate situations, make impact analysis, etc. to support decision making.

For historical and organizational reasons, the data needed by the managerial staff can reside in heterogeneous, distributed databases. EISs applications must be able

---

[30] Based on Orchestra Deliverable D.4.1.1 - MEIS Integration Report, authored by José António Frias, Software AG, and D 4.1.2 MEIS Plug Specification, authored by Gro Oftedal, Taskon

[31] D.4.1.1 - MEIS Integration Report. This report contains a fairly good review of the functionalities and methodologies associated with Executive Information Systems. It also reviews several existing products (Acumen Enterprise Solution, BusinessObjects, Commander, Express/EIS, Focus/EIS, Forest & Trees, Holos, Lightship, Lotus Notes, OnTrack, Power Play , SAS/EIS, Taskon Integrator).

to access these databases in a transparent way to the user, freeing him from the need of knowing where the data are and how they are physically organised. EISs are mostly developed using special EIS development tools or powerful 4GL tools with capabilities to meet EIS requirements.

MEIS/EIS for workflow based systems - WF-EIS. To be able to see MEIS/EIS in the context of Orchestra, we must define the characteristics of an EIS for workflow based systems, hereafter denoted WF-EIS. This represents an enhancement to traditional EISs in also extracting data from the workflow system and thereby bringing the business processes closer to the management. In addition to general EIS requirements, a WF-EIS must be able to:

- present essential knowledge of the workflow process model
- present information from the operative workflow management
- present combinations of workflow information and other management information

To achieve these results, one requires knowledge and access to the workflow process model and its operative environment. The value of having access to workflow information is related to the management's need to relate the business processes to strategic decisions. As pointed out in 'Workflow White Paper (R.T. Marshak): the challenge is in getting the right processes right, to achieve business goals.

Goals and Scope of the MEIS-Plug in Orchestra. An EIS presents management information. The specification of an EIS is heavily dependent upon the production systems of the enterprise. Similarly, the specification of a WF-EIS is dependent upon the target workflow system and possibly other systems with which it interacts (other workflow systems, invoked applications, etc.).

The goal for Orchestra was to specify a 'WF-EIS-plug' which can be used together with an EIS development tool to develop WF-EIS's. We will not elaborate on general requirements to EISs but rather refer to relevant literature where necessary. It was also a goal to be able to outline the main requirements to the interface against the workflow and sketch some combinations of workflow and management information.

We define a WF-EIS plug as a framework to facilitate the further development of a complete EIS with access to workflow information and production systems. An implemented WF-EIS plug will include an interface to a workflow system, and thereby an assumption of a certain workflow model. This specification uses the Orchestra workflow model as its basis, but the requirements are not restricted only to that model only. We have not considered interfaces/interaction against multiple workflow systems.

A WF-EIS plug will not contain any interfaces to the other enterprise information systems, but certainly give indications as to which kind of information it will be relevant to combine with the workflow information. The figure below gives some indication as to what parts of an EIS the plug will cover.

Figure 3-35. MEIS Plug integration approach

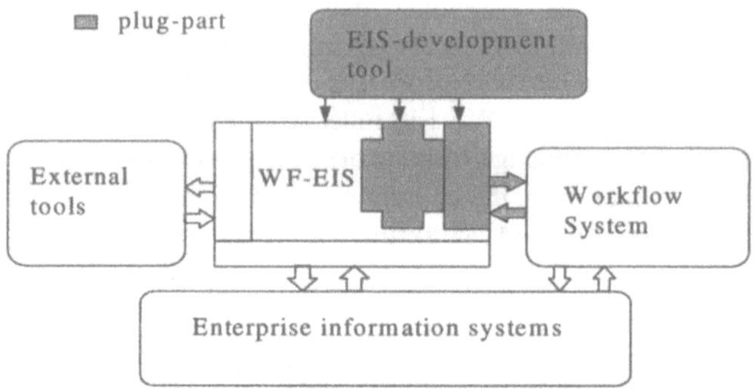

Using an implemented WF-EIS plug as a framework for the implementation of a full scale WF-EIS, there will be a need to:

- Elaborate the requirements for the total EIS system
- Develop EIS-specific functionality based on information needs and the enterprise information systems
- Adjust the interface to the workflow system
- Integrate the EIS-data with the workflow data
- Integrate external tools and applications.

The Orchestra WF-EIS features and functionality. The WF-EIS has been developed with the Taskon Integrator tool. Integrator allows a fast development of information-retrieval applications and an easy design of reports, charts, etc. Another advantage of this tool is that it can access to any database that supports standard SQL. As the Workflow data is stored in a relational-SQL database, the Workflow data is accessed directly using the Integrator tools.

The WF-MEIS user interface has been designed to be easy-to-use, making extensive use of mouse-selections, menus, etc. under the MS-Windows environment. Although integrated with Orchestra via Elenix, the WF-MEIS can also work as an independent module (except for the Workflow data that must be accessible). Following is a summary of the reports that can be generated:

- General (4): delayed processes, general statistics,...
- Persons (10): processes delayed more than X, stages,...
- Roles (11): persons who fill a role, pending processes,...
- Flows (14): stages, roles, delayed/pending/finished stages,...
- Processes (7): get attributes, roles involved.
- Stages (4): get attributes, actions, roles and transitions.
- Transitions (3): get attr., actions, get conditions/stages.

3.4.2 Interactive Negotiation Tools [32]

The construction of interactive negotiation tools or, as the perspective grew up, facilitation tools, had two dimensions in Orchestra. The first dimension has to do with the design and development of a suite of tools in the specific environment of Orchestra (Client/Server, Windows interfaces). While related tools exist, the requirements for integration with other components of Orchestra, as well as the wish to elaborate on the interaction approaches, led us to these developments. The second dimension relates with the problem, which fundamental nature became clearer and clearer along the project, of linking together support for regulated of formal processes (a long name for traditional workflow) and support for informal and ad-hoc decision processes. This problem, rooted on the conviction that real life work processes are neither purely formal nor purely unregulated, has been addressed in the scope of this line of work in Orchestra. As we will see, the recognition of this problem and its analysis probably created more open issues that real solutions.

Indeed, helps to decision making can fundamentally be of two types. Those that have to be made by agreement with other members of the group, or those that have to be made by only one person. It is not always clearly defined when it has to be by one or the other way for the people who have to assume the responsibility of the decision. In the case of group decisions, in many occasions, it is not clear either how to handle the situations.

Then we can see two essential components which have guided the development of this module in the ORCHESTRA Project. There are types of problems, depending on their origin or nature, and thus they require different processings. The studies directed towards the classification and processing of the diverse types of problems represented by the diverse types of situations within an organisation, are carried out by the so-called Contingency Models. Among the best known, three have

[32] Based on Orchestra Deliverable D 4.2.1 - Negotiation Subsystem: Integrating Workflow with Group Decision Techniques, authored by Pedro Antunes, Javier Segovia, Nuno Guimarães, and Jesus Cardeñosa, INESC and UPMadrid.

been selected for the Project, to estimate that together they are able to represent or deal with the greatest part of the situations that can occur in an organisation. These Contingency Models are the Thompson [Cardeñosa 96], Vroom [Vroom 88] and Stumpf [Stumpf 79] models.

On the other hand, there are decision making help techniques, some are individual an others group techniques. Many of them were already described in Deliverable 4.2.1. "Negotiation Subsystem: Integrating Workflow with Group Decision Techniques". For the Negotiation Subsystem module of the ORCHESTRA Project, three of them (Voting, Brainstorming and Nominal Group Technique) were selected and developed as they were considered as the more significant and effective for group decisions in organisations.

The system of the ORCHESTRA Project integrates the two means and is formed by the following systems:

- Analysis Subsystem: in charge of studying the problems using the Contingency Models and suggesting the more adequate decision technique/s for this problem.
- Decision Subsystem: able to select the more adequate technique and to apply it through the communication to the members of the group (call up a meeting automatically) besides to prepare the training of the group, each of the members acting from their posts for the decision making. This process required the use of the features of the Elenix although particularly of the capacities of the Client-server architecture for the process articulation.

For the system to be able to carry out these two tasks, two additional operating modules are necessary:

- Tool Manager: in charge of fulfilling the recommendations of the Analysis Subsystem as for the selection of the technique to apply as well as the management of its application. Then they interact with the Decision Subsystem and the Tool Bench that we describe below.
- Tool Bench: This module is the one which "contains" the different decision tools, in this case NGT, Voting and Brainstorming. The incorporation of new decision tools should be done incorporating them to this module.

On the following we show the aspect for the user of the analysis system as well as the application of one of the techniques.

Figure 3-36 Analysis system: Main Window

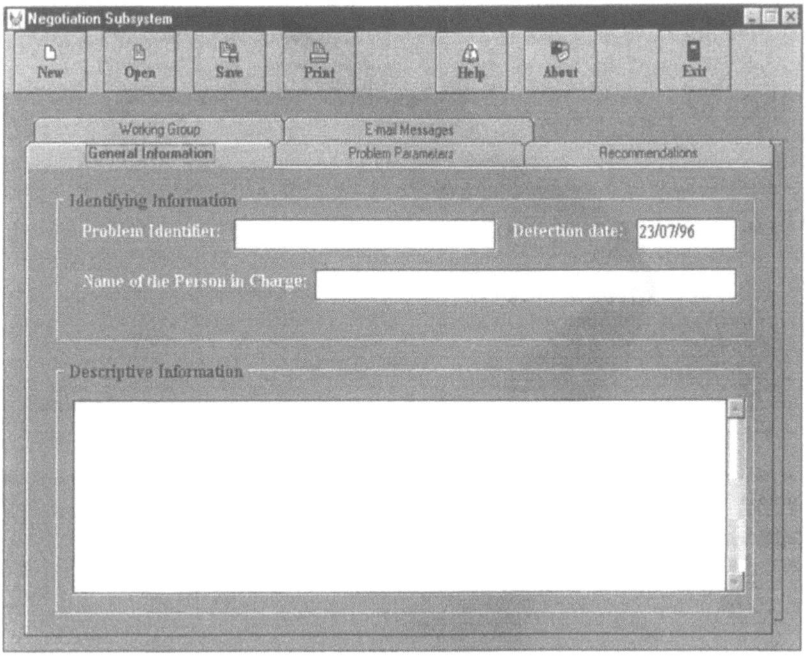

Figure 3-37. Analysis System: Parameters Window

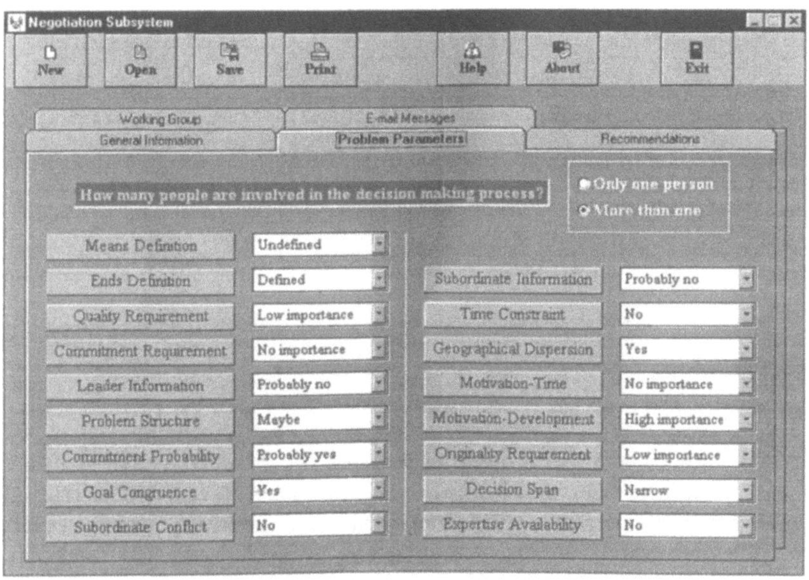

Figure 3-38. Analysis System: Recommendations Window

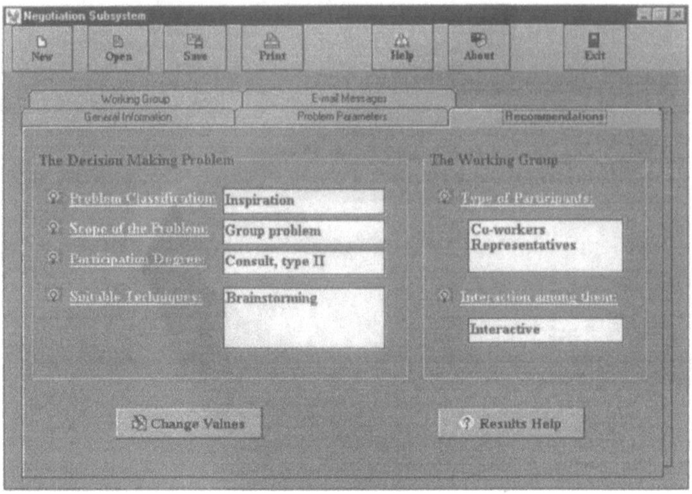

Figure 3-39. Sample View of Negotiation Tools

The above picture illustrates the main aspects of the interactive negotiation & decision tools that have been designed in Orchestra. The relevant aspects are: (1) Direct manipulation interface; (2) Consistency of interface across several techniques (Brainstorming, Voting, Nominal Group Technique); (3) Integration with the remainder of the Negotiation subsystem and with Orchestra as a whole.

4. Architectural Issues in Orchestra

This chapter presents a set of architectural issues of the Orchestra environment. As mentioned several times in the previous chapters, the results of the Orchestra project will not necessarily lead to a unique system with a fixed packaging choice. On the contrary, it is expected (and this is reflected in the partners' exploitation plans) that several configurations of the Orchestra modules be designed, refined and (probably) reengineered, to address specific needs and commercial goals.

This chapter presents the full map and logical relations among the macroscopic components of Orchestra. Additionally, it presents the architectural configurations that implement the functionality described in the previous chapter. An important set of information related with the architecture of the Orchestra environment are the mechanisms for modularity that are included further in this chapter. By mechanisms
for modularity, we mean essentially available interfaces between modules, Application Programmer's Interfaces, and file or database specifications for information interchange. These should be observed as proposals, preliminary mechanisms based on the prototyping efforts, and not certified interfaces, or commitments from the partners in the Orchestra.

4.1 Logical Architecture [33]

The logical architecture of the ORCHESTRA system is depicted in fig. 4.1. The figure identifies the main modules of the Orchestra system (topdown):

[33] Based on Technical Annex and Progress Reports 1,2,3 and reflecting final status.

User Environment Layer

- Document management (Archive) system
- Document Generation system
- Other applications (like Correspondence Log, Agenda, Fax, EMail, etc.)

Service Layer

- Workflow management services
- Contextual Communication services
- Decision and Negotiation support services

Infrastructural Layer

- Security services
- Integration of external Database Systems and Servers
- Communication, Messaging and directory services

Figure 4-1. Generic Orchestra Logical Architecture

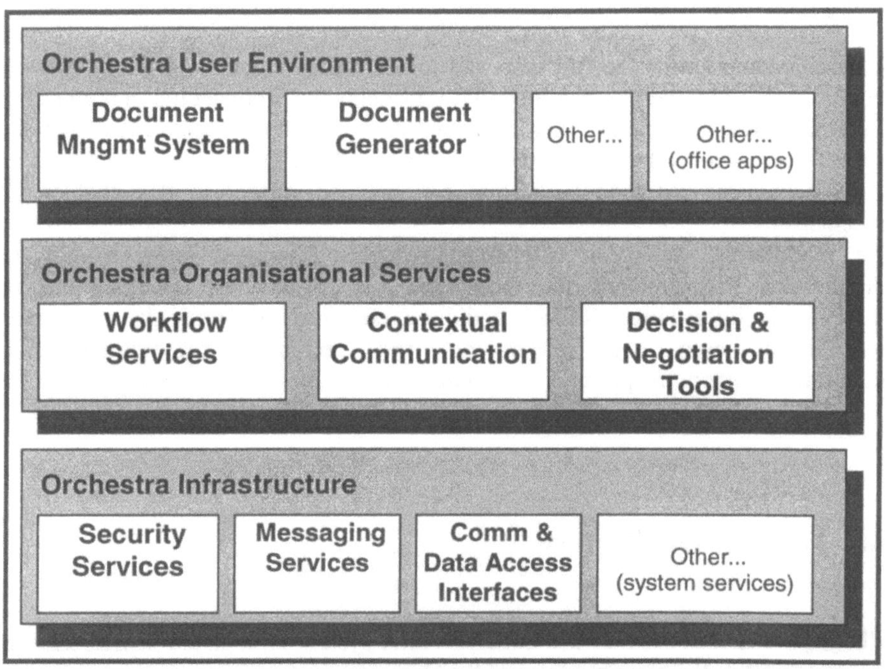

The blocks represented above interact in several ways and due to multiple needs. These interactions are described on a per-system basis in the following sections. On the other hand, this representation of a logical architecture does no reflect the client-server separation that is intrinsic to most of the modules. In fact the typical module has a client interface (even if only for administration purposes - the case of the Contextual Communication Services) where the user functionality is reflected, and a server component, located (typically) in the Unix machine used as server. This separation will be apparent in the following discussion.

4.2 Specific Architectural Configurations

The following subsections present the main architectural characteristics of the several Orchestra components. Technical details are omitted in most cases and left to a specific chapter that follows.

4.2.1 Document Archive Architecture

The architecture of the Orchestra Document Archive has been designed with a fundamental concern for a gradual and sustained evolution of the Elenix Multimedia Document Archive. To meet this engineering requirements, the new functionality was incorporated in a new type of Archive designated as Remote-secure. This new type of Archive system coexists with already existing Local and Remote archive types.

The figure below represents the architecture for the server (on the right side) and client (on the left side) parts of the Remote-Secure (RS) Archive.

Figure 4-2 Remote-secure document archive architecture

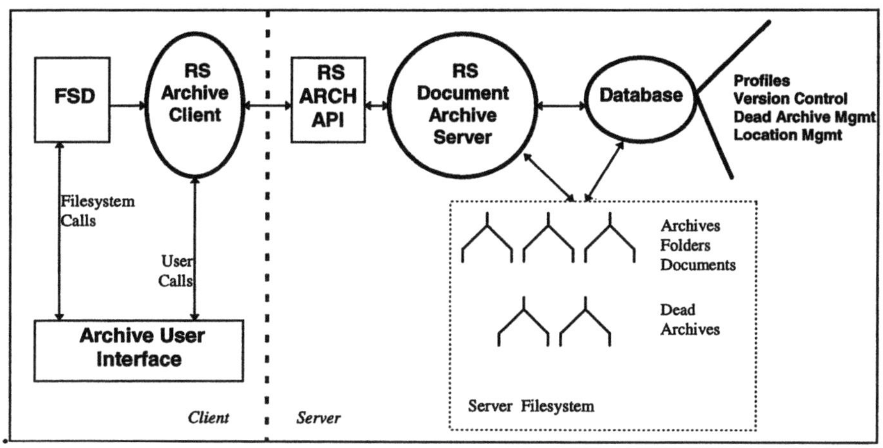

Server Component. The Remote-secure archive resides on the server. The server is UNIX or Windows NT. It uses the server file system to map Archives, folders and documents on directories and files. There is database support to store the Profile data, the Version Control data, the Dead Archive Management data, and the Location Management data. This data is associated to the Archives, folders and documents in the file system.

The RS Document Archive Server manages and maintains the archives, folders and documents in the filesystem, as well as their coherence with the information in the database. The RS Archive API provides the functions required to store and retrieve archives, folders and documents, as well as to query and edit some of the information in the database.

Client Component. The target working environment for the client component of the Archive was Windows 95 and Windows NT. In order to provide as much transparency as possible, the archive, either local or remote, is accessed through a dedicated device driver (FSD in the picture above). These new operating systems already offer a specification for such device-drivers. An implementation based on real-mode device drivers as used in SunSoft PC-NFS (for DOS) was discarded due to the expected life time of Windows 3.1x

Windows 95 and Windows NT offer a set of APIs to implement multiple file systems, what is referred to as the Installable File System (IFS). The IFS uses a special loadable device driver, called File System Driver (FSD), which can be loaded only when a file name is resolved. FSD´s interact with IFS manager via a C interface.

Conceptually, this FSD will interact with the RS Document Archive Client. This module is responsible for the communication with the RS Document Archive Server, through the RS Document Archive API. The RS Document Archive Client also supports functionality not related with the FSD I/O working. This functionality, the "User calls", may comprehend actions like : checking in a document for version control, filling data for the document profile, displaying the results of a document search, etc. This device driver solution offers great transparency and independence for operations with block scope; the "User Calls" will provide operations with higher level than block scope.

In addition to the I/O functionality it must offer to the Windows IFS Manager, this device driver is responsible for:

- sending logged users credentials and location info in a secure format (ticket and authentication supplied by the Security subsystem) on a per request basis,
- decrypt received blocks with the logged user key,
- encrypt blocks to be written with the logged user key.

A different FSD may offer the same functionality to a local file system based archive. Only a local user can use it though.

Intermediate Architecture An intermediate stage during the development circumvented the Device Driver approach. This stage is presented in figure 4.

Figure 4-3. Intermediate stage for the Remote-secure document archive - client

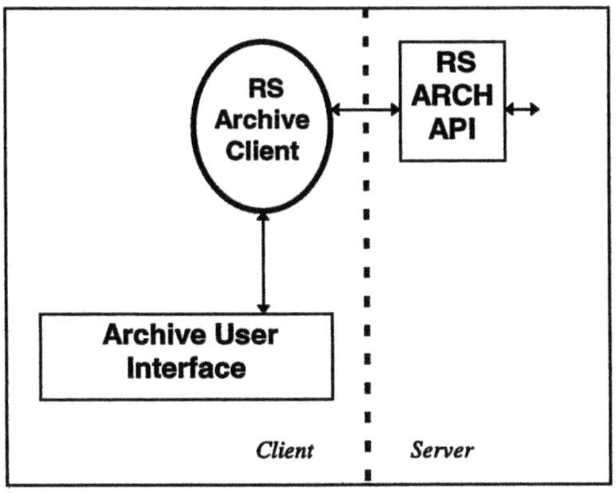

In the intermediate stage, the FSD is not present, thus sacrificing transparency during I/O and the integrated encryption/decryption of file blocks. The only RS Document Archive Client inputs are "User calls". In practice, a Document Archive prototype running according to this intermediate architecture presents the following characteristics :

- documents are transferred from the server to the client PC when the user accesses them and stored on a temporary file,
- decryption is applied to the document as a whole, and the decrypted document will be stored on the PC disk,
- encryption of the document is made on user demand,
- the user is responsible to register the document, causing its transference back to the server;
- all I/O is made through the built-in device drivers.

This approach allows for a version of the Archive system that is able to run on Windows 3.1x (both single user version and Windows for WorkGroups).

4.2.2 Document Generator Architecture

The process of generating a certain document merges two kinds of information:

- the **document template**, the static part of the document (i.e. the blank form),
- the **dynamic information** (for example, the contents of the fields in a form).

This merge occurs according to a **set of rules**, associated to the type of document. The figure below shows the scheme of the basic document generation process.

Figure 4-4. - Basic Document Generator Modules

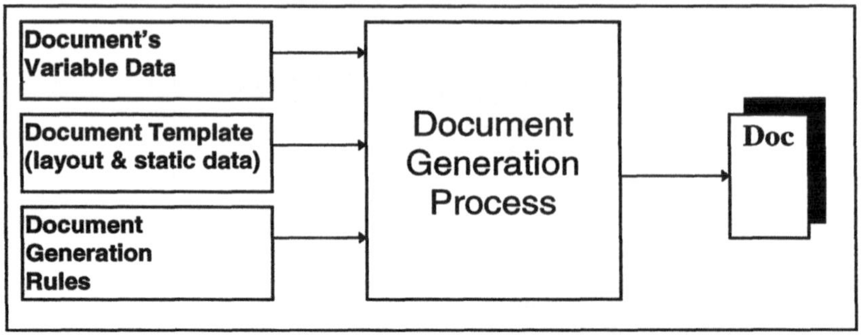

The inputs to the document generation process are the document template, the document's variable information, and the set of rules that regulate the generation. Some other sources of input are added to the document generation process:

- User supplied dynamic information, for interactive document generation,
- Dynamic information acquired from information subsystem, for automatic generation of several instances of the same document type based on data stored in the corporate database,
- an interface with the workflow management subsystem, since the document generator often acts as a front-end to this subsystem,
- The generator also interfaces with the user environment.

The architecture for the Document Generator is represented in the figure below.

Figure 4-5. Complete Document Generator Architecture

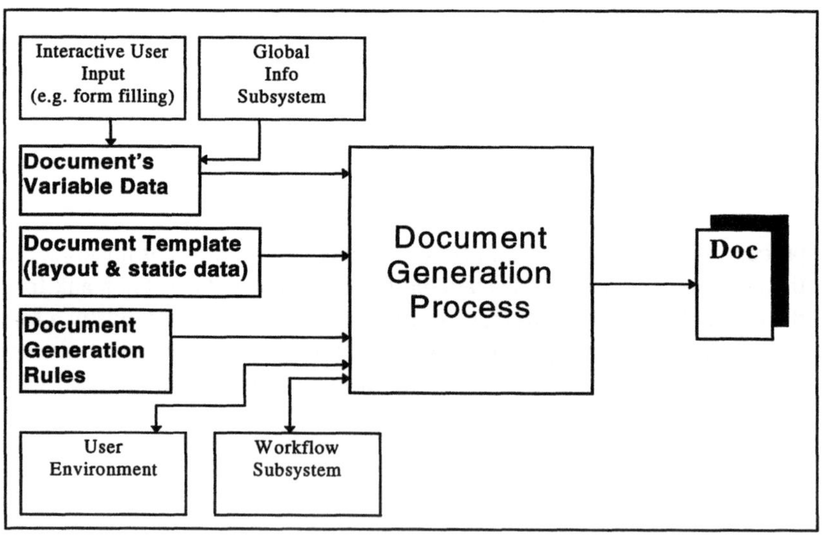

The Document Generator uses the Rules to merge the Document Template with the Document's Variable Information, obtained from the user or the Information subsystem. The Document Template acts as the starting point of the generation process. The following activities are the responsibility of the Document Generator:

1. From the Document Template, obtain the set of Document Generation Rules that correspond to the type of document (template) in question,
2. Validate the user's right to generate the type of document in question,
3. Interpret & apply the Doc Generation Rules, merging template and variable data,
4. During the merging process: generate queries to the user or to the Information subsystem, to obtain the variable data; If the generation process is interactive, validate or restrict the user's right to fill in (or even read) some parts of the document; communicate with the workflow subsystem or other services to obtain information needed to apply the rules;
5. build the output document.

The detailed architecture is depicted in the following figure. The Document Generator is composed of 7 building blocks, described below:

- **Document Template**. Contains the document layout and static information (text, images, logos, etc.), as well as information concerning the set of rules that apply to this document template. In form filling, the document template corresponds to the blank form and contains information on how to obtain the set of rules that determine field filling.
- **Document Generation Rules** Interprets the rules associated with the template. Communicates with the Rules Server, to validate the user's right to apply the rules.
- **Rules Server** Manages the Document Generation Rules. The rules are kept in the RS Document Archive for security reasons. Any request to apply a rule is evaluated by the Rules Server. Also controls concurrent modification of rules.
- **Variable Data Acquisition** Takes care of the interaction between the Document Generator and the variable data sources (user or information subsystem). Requests information from the user, and generates queries to the Information subsystem.
- **Document Builder** Creates and formats the output document. The document builder is able to read the template, and build the output document from then on.
- **Template Editor** Supports interactive creation and editing of the templates. Templates are stored in the RS Document Archive. The rights to access/modify the edited templates are checked by the Archive.
- **Rules Editor & Compiler** Supports the creation, editing, and test of the document generation rules. Its output are rules that become known when registered in the Rules Server and stored in the RS Document Archive. The

user's privileges to access/modify the edited rules are validated through the Rules Server.

Figure 4-6. Detailed Document Generator Architecture

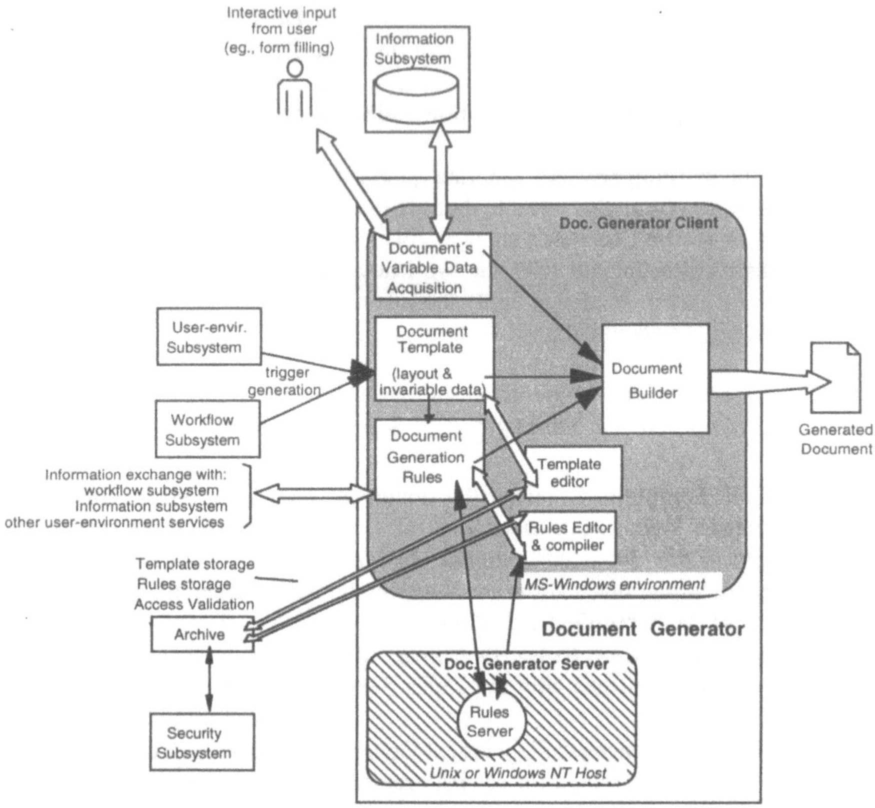

4.2.3 Workflow Engine Architecture

The workflow system architecture, depicted below shows three main interacting components :

- The Flow drawing application
- The Form design application
- The Workflow client application

These are Windows based client applications that interact with the workflow kernel part of the ELENIX Multimedia server through several API's (presented in the Appendices to this report).

Figure 4-7. Workflow System Architecture

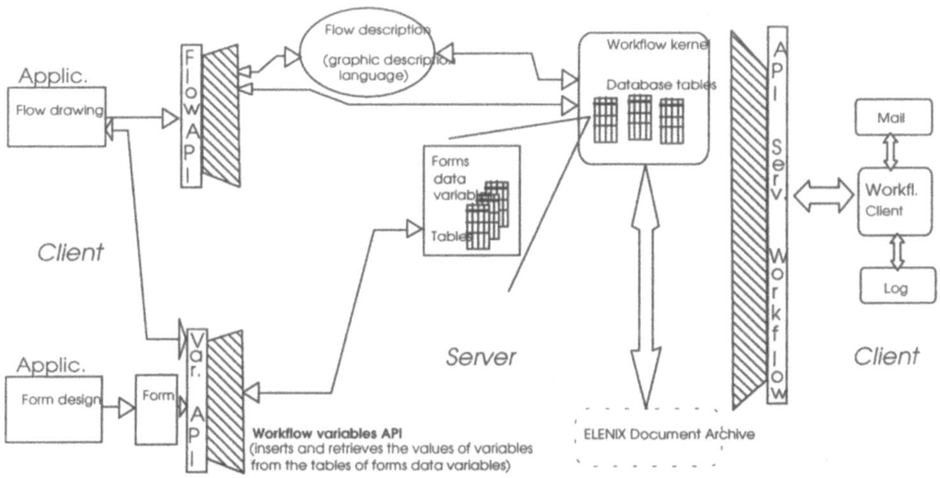

The Flow drawing application runs on the client PC, and is used to graphically define the flow paths, variables, and content of stages, tasks and conditions. This application interacts with the workflow kernel (via the Flow API) in three ways :

- The description for the flow (described with the graphical description language) defines object types (start stage, stage, end stage, conditions and joins), coordinates and links that constitute the flow. This file, associated to a flow, is transferred to the server and registered in the Orchestra/Elenix 3.0 document archive. Although not clear from the figure, the Flow drawing application is invoked via OLE 2.0 by the Client application. Besides the already mentioned flow creation, it is also used to view and modify already running processes.
- Non-graphical data defining flows (e.g. content of stages, specific tasks, etc) is passed via the Flow API to the workflow kernel.
- The third type of interaction addresses the definition of variables associated with flows. These user defined variables constitute the flow specific data. For this purpose, the Flow drawing application interacts with the Variables API, that, on their turn, are stored in the database tables of the Workflow kernel.

The Form design application is based on third-party products. The forms provide access to the variables associated with a process. This access is made through the already mentioned Variables API. This allows for great flexibility on the choice of the forms tool, the only requisite being the ability invoke functions from an external DLL.

The Workflow client application allows the typical workflow type of interaction: process dispatching, stage transition, task execution, process search, etc.. This application uses the Workflow API to interact with the workflow kernel.

4.2.4 Security Architecture

Figure 4-8. Architecture of the Security system (client-left, server-right)

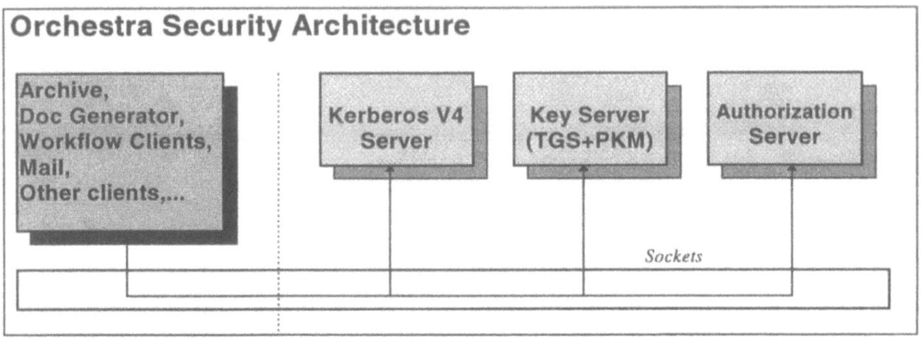

Authentication Service

1. Authenticates users in the login protocol.
2. Generates initial user's credentials to access other system services.
3. Checks user's credentials.
4. Manages a record of all successful attempts to login or logout the system.

Key Service

1. Acts as a trusted third-party in the generation and distribution of shared secret keys between two or more communicating peers.
2. Maintains the history of all user's public keys used and still in use.
3. Acts as a Certification Authority, as defined by X.509. It is responsible for managing, distributing and checking user public keys and user certificates (signed data structures with user identification and public keys).
4. Generates and checks user signatures.

Secure e-mail

1. Generic PEM filters to manage PEM messages. These filters can be used by applications exchanging mail-like messages (e.g. FAX). PEM is independent from h/w architectures, operating systems and communication protocols, is compatible with several key management policies and provides data confidentiality and integrity, authentication and non-repudiation of sender.
2. Secure e-mail introducing PEM filters in the mail reception and delivery.chain

Secure RPC.

1. An RPC package allowing mutual peer authenticity, privacy of message headers and data, data integrity and protocol integrity.

4.2.5 Global Information System Architecture

The architecture of the "Global Information System" has no specific characteristics apart from those derived from the use of the Software AG's ENTIRE middleware services. The Global Information system provides connectivity interfaces and data access and manipulation performance which are capable of working in the overall ORCHESTRA architecture:

Figure 4-9. Architecture of the Global Information system

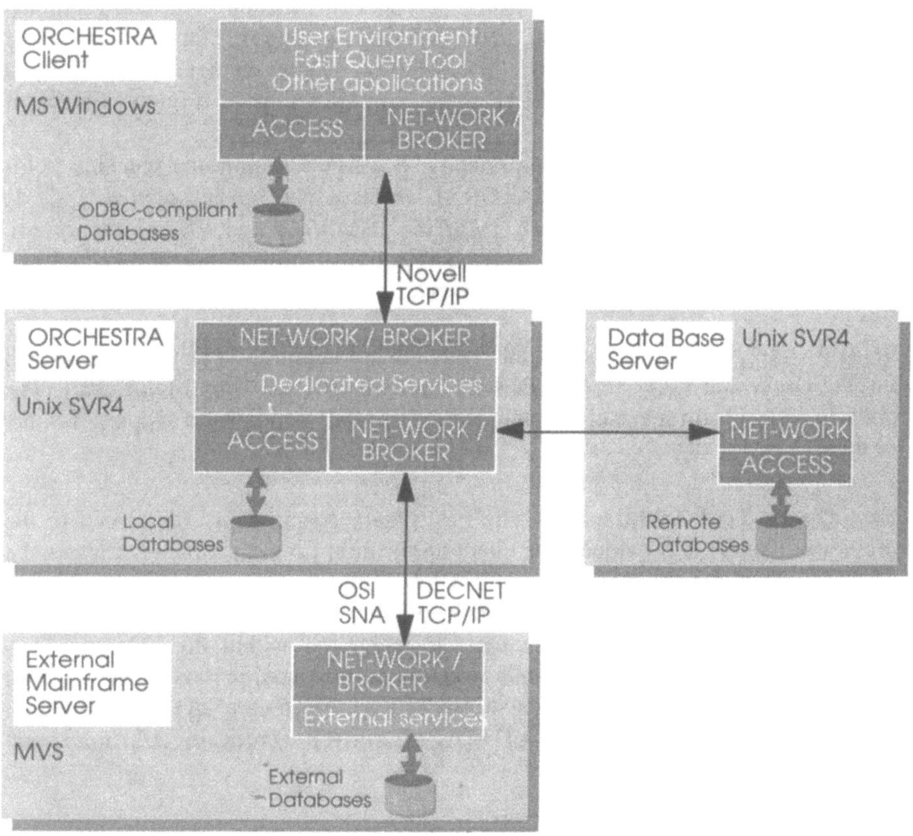

The examples that were prepared to demonstrate this functionality were the following:

1. Access to a database located in a mainframe, and subsequent map generation (based on Document Generator package)
2. Access to a generic facilities management database, and test of the Fast Query system.

- ORCHESTRA client: The User Environment runs in a PC workstation under MS Windows. Data Access and Manipulation System provides a direct interface, via ENTIRE ACCESS, to local ODBC-compliant databases from NATURAL.
- ORCHESTRA server: Dedicated servers are located in a UNIX machine. The dedicated services are able to access the local relational databases via ENTIRE ACCESS. (ORACLE, INFORMIX, INGRES, SYBASE, DB2/6000, and ADABAS supported). NET-WORK and BROKER assure client-server connectivity.
- Data Base Server: Additional UNIX servers can be connected, and relational data bases accessed. Again, NET-WORK provides connectivity, while ENTIRE ACCESS supports accessibility. Data access is performed transparently from the NATURAL services in the server, as if remote databases were linked locally.
- External Mainframe Server: Optionally, if a MVS Mainframe machine holds other corporate databases, NATURAL services can be designed to provide direct access (ADABAS; DB2, IMS/DB, IDMS/DB and VSAM supported). NET-WORK and BROKER assure connectivity and interoperability between Server and the External Mainframe Server.

Several widely used communication protocols are supported (TCP/IP and Novell for PC-Unix, and OSI, SNA, DECNET and TCP/IP for Unix-Mainframe). The underlying transport mechanism included in ENTIRE middleware supports for any of them.

Fast Query Tool Architecture. The Fast Query functionality (described in the previous chapter) is provided by a client application program which harnesses the ENTIRE client-server approach in the Global Information system for accessing without taking into account their DBMS's to either local databases or remote ones. This application -the Fast Query tool- is integrated within the ORCHESTRA environment. The Fast Query module structure is illustrated in next figure. All Fast Query modules have been written in NATURAL (Software AG 4th generation programming language) and NATURAL EXPERT (Software AG functional programming language).

Figure 4-10. Fast Query Tool Architecture

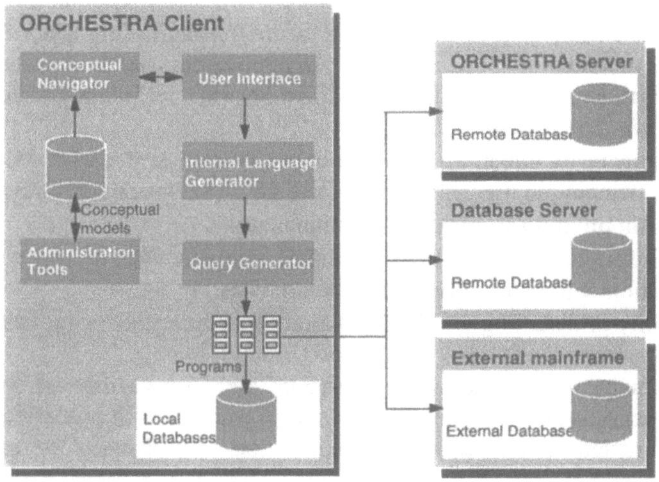

4.2.6 MAPI Integration

The MAPI architecture is designed to make it easy to write messaging-enabled applications that are independent of the messaging system. To do this, MAPI provides two "faces": the application program interfaces (client APIs), which form the client-to-MAPI link, and the service-provider interfaces, which complete the MAPI-to-messaging system link. MAPI provides a set of function calls that, act as brokers between the front-end (client) applications and the back-end (network-messaging) system. This dual interface helps ensure true openness on both the client and server sides. Using MAPI calls, any messaging application can use any messaging service. The application developers are freed from the messaging-system concerns. MAPI's architecture provides separate APIs for both the client applications (front end) and for the messaging systems (back end), allowing true independence between the two.

Figure 4-11 - Architecture of the Messaging mechanisms (client-left, server-right)

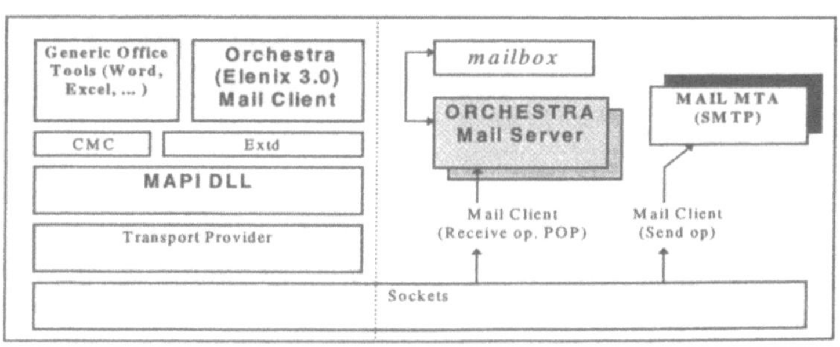

4.2.7 Contextual Communication Architecture

The decisions concerning the architecture of the Formalization, Classification and Distribution modules of the Contextual Communication Services were subject to several considerations related to Client/Server technology, adopted by ORCHESTRA. These were:

- Development of either a Client module (located in the user PC), a Server module (running in the UNIX or Mainframe server machine), or both.
- Options in program-to-program communication.
- Nature of user interaction (conversational or non-conversational execution).
- Connection with other ORCHESTRA modules.
- Possibility of installing the F&C&D module as independent applications.

The Contextual Communication modules (F&C and Distribution) are configured as centralized servers, and provide a set of callable routines with predefined input and output parameters. Client-server Communication is performed by means of an Remote Procedure Call (RPC) mechanism. The main reasons that led to this decision were:

Figure 4-12. Contextual Communication Architecture

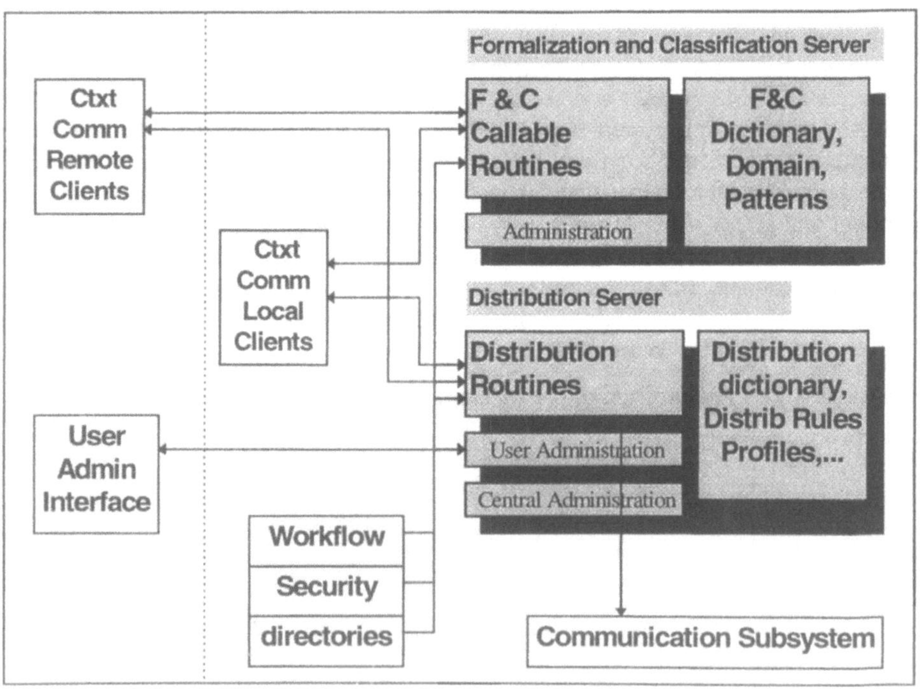

- **Accessibility:** The F&C and Distribution Servers, running in a UNIX or mainframe server machine, are accessible from all other ORCHESTRA modules.
- **Integration:** The RPC mechanism is the simplest way to allow an easy integration
- **Performance:** This schema is optimal for an efficient real-time response, and also supports batch processes.
- **User interaction:** The drawback is the need to design a request-response execution protocol
- Finally, the administration module will be centralized. The current prototype will not include any callable function for distributed administration.

Other relevant aspects, more specific to the Distribution mechanisms, are:

- The Distribution Routines is accessible from local clients (located in the same server machine) as well as remote clients. For instance, the client applications using the Formalisation and Classification module can also be the clients of the Distribution Routines, since the output of the F&C module is the input of the Distribution Machine. Also, the Communication Subsystem can make use of the F&C module and the Distribution module (Communication Filter Subsystem) in order to examine and redirect received messages.
- The User Administration Service is separated into a client side and a server side, in order to incorporate a user-friendly interface. The client side will be installed on every ORCHESTRA client workstation using the distribution machine, and will consist on the required Graphical User Interface for the definition of distribution rules, user preferences and other user-dependent aspects involved in the distribution.
- The server side interacts with the client side via a RPC mechanism, and will perform the actions specified in the client. In this case, the Remote Procedure Call strategy is also the best conjunction of efficiency and simplicity to achieve the functionality required for the User Administration facilities.
- Finally, the Central Administration Service tools for the maintenance of Receiver Entities and other system information will be centralized, and located entirely on the server machine. The access to the Central Administration interface will be performed via direct terminals or PC emulation. Since the Central Administration services will normally be accessed by a reduced group of users, the development of a Graphical User Interface is not foreseen in this case.

Integration with other ORCHESTRA subsystems. This section presents the main aspects related to the interaction of the Contextual Communication module with other ORCHESTRA subsystems.

The F&C functions will be called by the User Environment and the Informal Communication subsystems. Therefore, these subsystems will perform as clients of the F&C server. On the other hand, the F&C functions will internally make use of Security, Workflow and Directory functions, that will be considered as servers for the F&C module.

- **User Environment and Informal Communication.** These subsystems are two of the users of the F&C subsystem. The mail system uses the F&C functions to process received messages or common mail-boxes. The fax server, assumed that an OCR system is available, formalizes and classifies received fax transmissions and, for instance, notify inferred addressees via E-mail. For letters and closed documents process, a simple module can be developed to prompt the user to enter information printed in the envelope.
- **Workflow.** Some information from the Workflow subsystem (rules and data) is useful to classify documents. There are two different ways of obtain data: accessing directly to the Workflow structures or loading data and rules in the Workflow subsystem into its own F&C module structures. In order to have a F&C module as independent as possible, the Workflow information is loaded on the F&C data structure. So, it is better to define in this module its own data structure to contain the information stored on the workflow instead of using direct calls only valid to this system (project). With this strategy, the F&C module could use information from different Workflow systems just changing the loading processes.
- **Directory services.** The information about people and resources of an organization is necessary for the F&C and Distribution modules to determine the people interested in a document. The F&C module will consider that Directory provided by the Informal Communication Subsystem is unique and complete. Large organizations usually have a distributed Directory. Every division or department has its own Directory; so if the F&C and Distribution modules only access a partial Directory, documents sometimes will not be properly classified or distributed. Also in this case, the maintenance and synchronization of an internal Directory structure can be considered. The main reasons supporting this option are the better performance in Directory search and the relatively-static nature of Directory information (daily loads can be acceptable for synchronization. The Contextual Communication module stores the corporate following the recommendation X.500 for directories. Consequently, the integration within legacy corporate X.500 directory will be very simple.

Figure 4-13. Normalization and Classification module decomposition

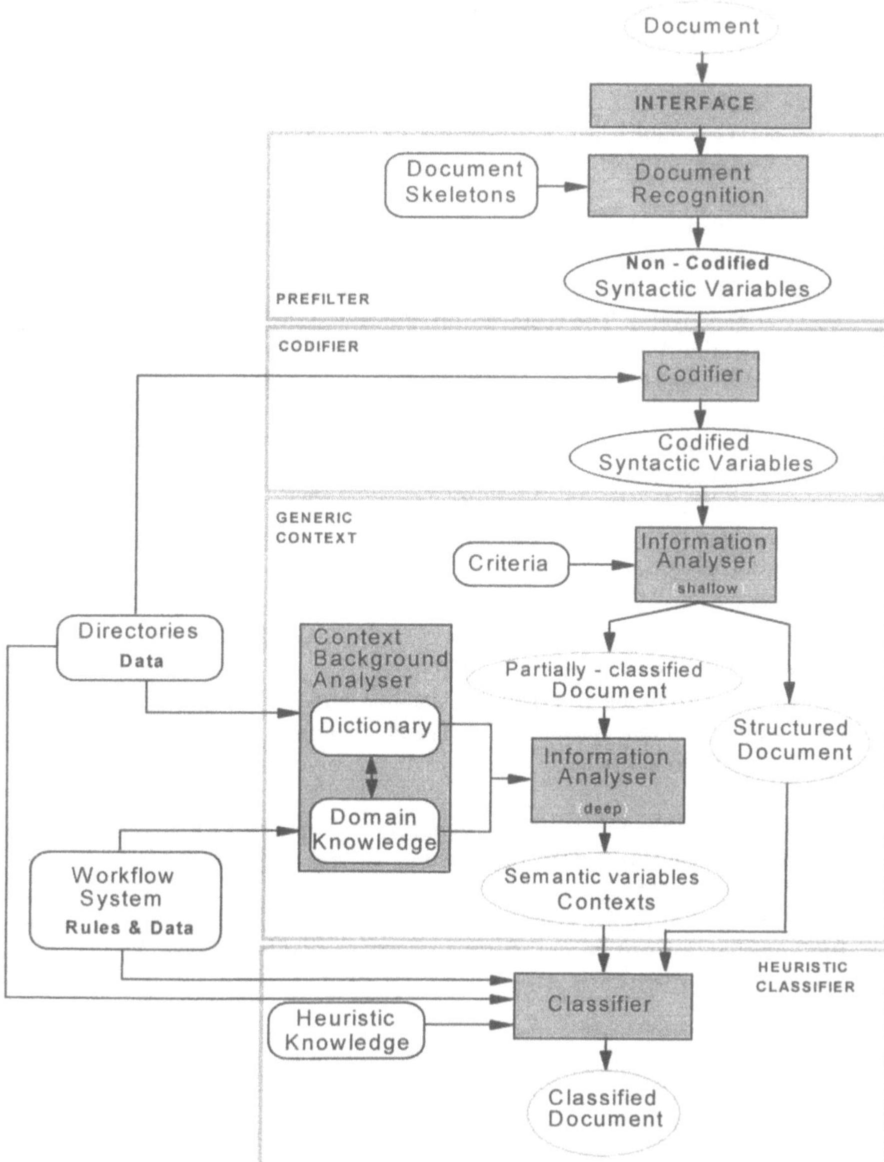

The Distribution module is called by the User Environment Subsystem, or accessed through the F&C module. These are clients of the Distribution server. The Distribution functions make use of Workflow and Directory functions, as well as the mail facilities provided by the Communication Subsystem. These modules are servers for the Distribution Machine. Finally, the connectivity mechanisms for client and server modules will be provided by the Connectivity interfaces of the *ORCHESTRA* Global Information Subsystem.

- **User Environment Subsystem**: Since the mail and fax servers will be accessible, the User Environment Subsystem itself includes the corresponding functions to call the Contextual Communication facilities, to distribute received message(s). The received fax transmissions can be forwarded to the Communication Filter Subsystem only in text mode, that is, assumed that an OCR tool is available.
- **Directory and Workflow:** Receiver Entities will be generated by the Distribution Machine using the information held from the Directory and Workflow (person names, addresses, jobs, groups, projects, responsibilities, and others). So, the Receiver Entities are a set of pre-processed internal data structures that represent the Directory and Workflow information relevant for distribution purposes.
- **Communication Subsystem:** The mail system can use the Distribution module to send to the right addressee the received E-mail messages or document stored on the common mailboxes.

  On the other hand, the Distribution Machine will also use the mail service of the Communication Subsystem to send received documents to selected addressees, or to notify them that they have receive a document and where it is located.
- **Connectivity interfaces:** The client/server communication infrastructure, including client and server registration, service request, data sending and reception, monitoring, tracing and others, will be provided by the ORCHESTRA Global Information Subsystem. By means of such facilities, a RPC mechanism will be enabled for access to the Distribution Routines and communication between User Administration Service client and server modules.

Figure 4-14. Distribution Machine module decomposition

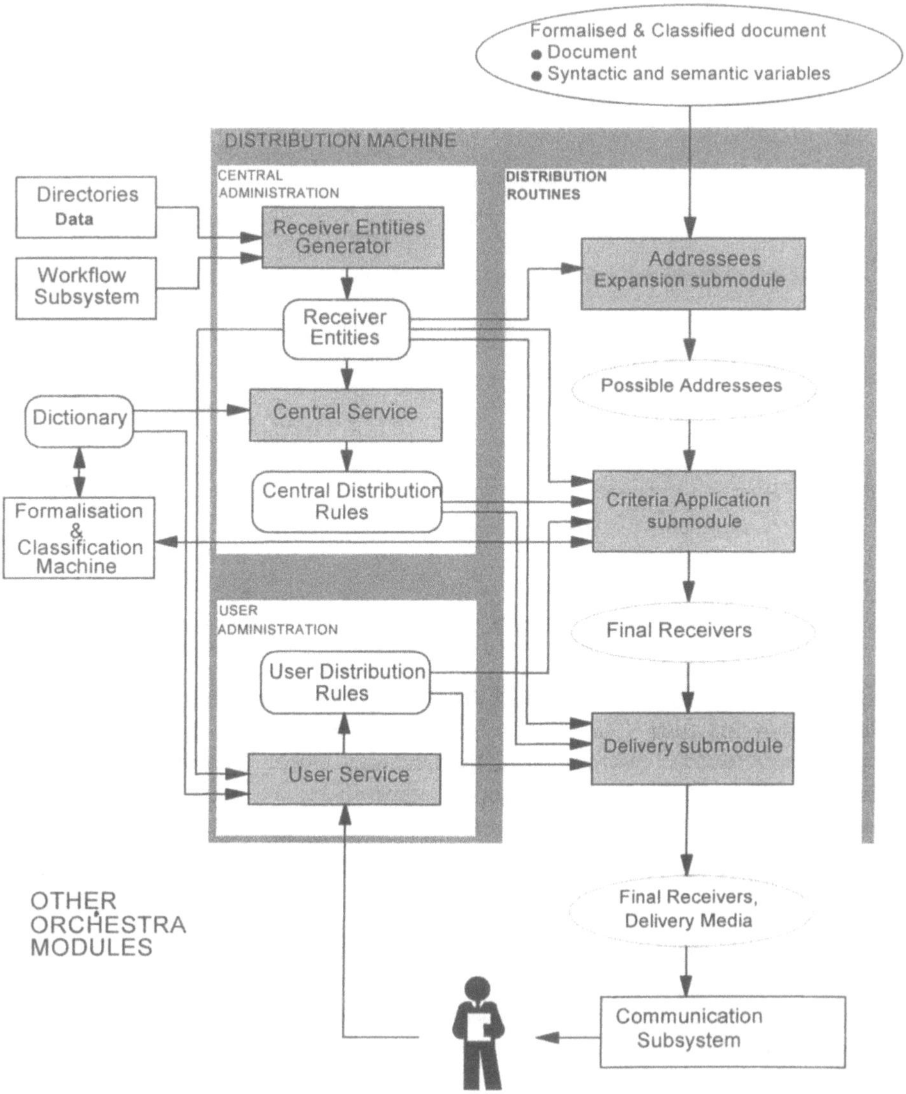

4.2.8 MEIS Plug Architecture

The architecture of the WF-EIS created for Orchestra is depicted on the next figure:

Figure 4-15. Orchestra MEIS Tool architecture

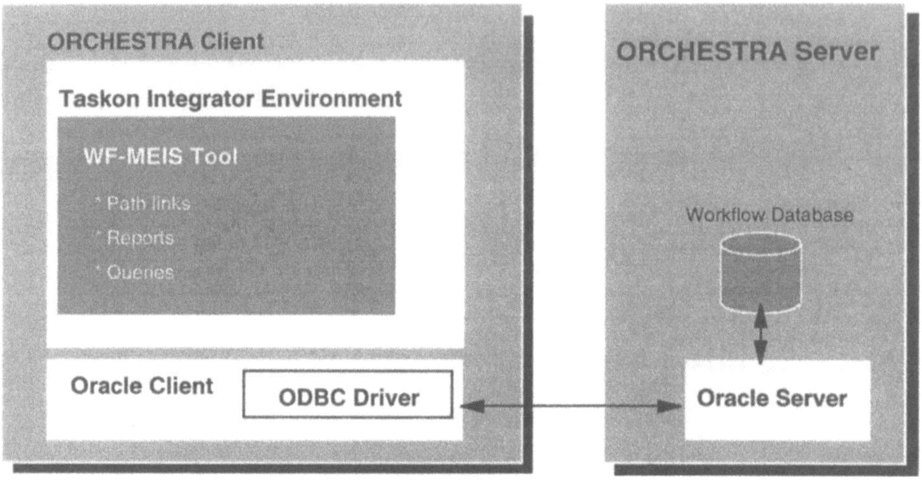

As shown in the figure, the MEIS Tool has been successfully adapted to the Orchestra architecture. The Taskon/Integrator can be used both as development tool and as a runtime environment at the Orchestra Client Windows 3.11 platform. On the other hand, the data access capabilities of the Taskon/Integrator environment allow to easily access to the Workflow Database, running on the Orchestra Server platform, by means of ODBC standard mechanisms.

4.2.9 Interactive Negotiation Tools Architecture

The generic architecture of the interactive negotiation tools designed for Orchestra is presented in the figure below:

This representation highlights the process by which these tools become integrated in the overall Orchestra environment.

- The beginning of the action of the Negotiation System is based on the detection of a problem within the organisation. The problem can be detected observing an interruption of the Workflow, or by an user with responsibilities.
- Once a "problem" is encountered, the Negotiation System proceeds along four fundamental functional modules:
    - Analysis Subsystem
    - Decision Subsystem
    - Tool Manager
    - Tool Bench

Figure 4-16. Global Architecture of the Negotiation Subsystem

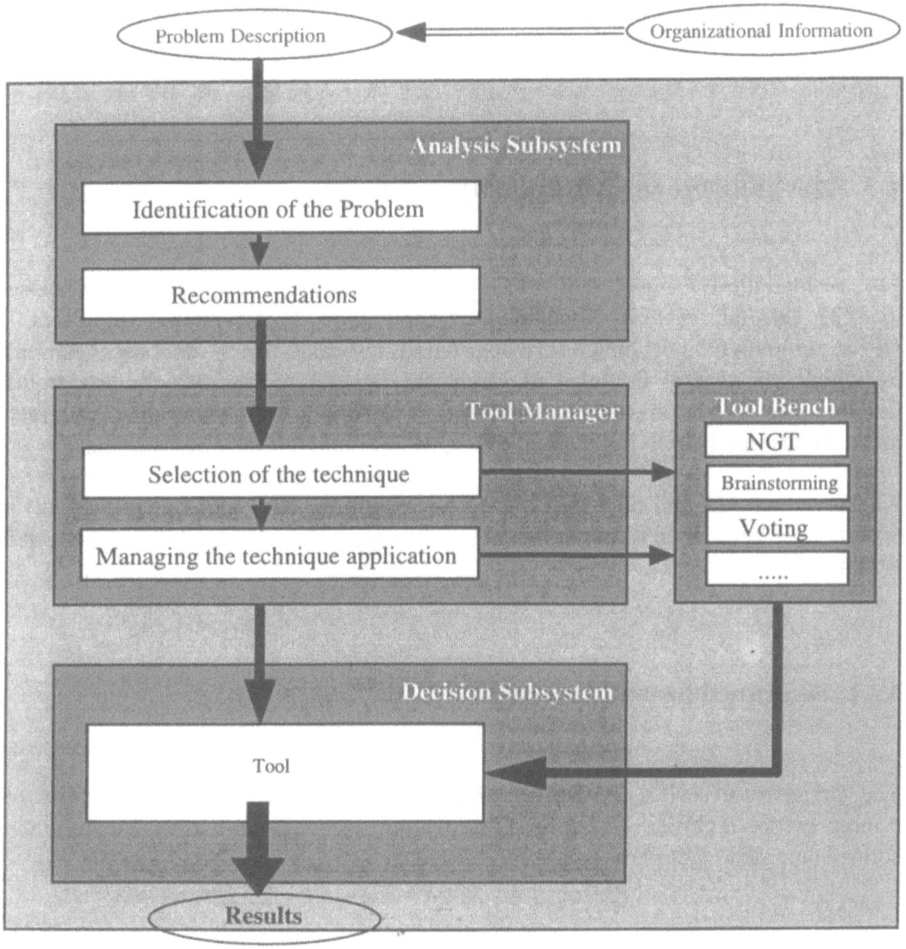

The interaction between them and the functions it carries out are clearly shown in the graph. The acting scheme according to the client-server architecture is the following.

Figure 4-17. Client-Server Architecture

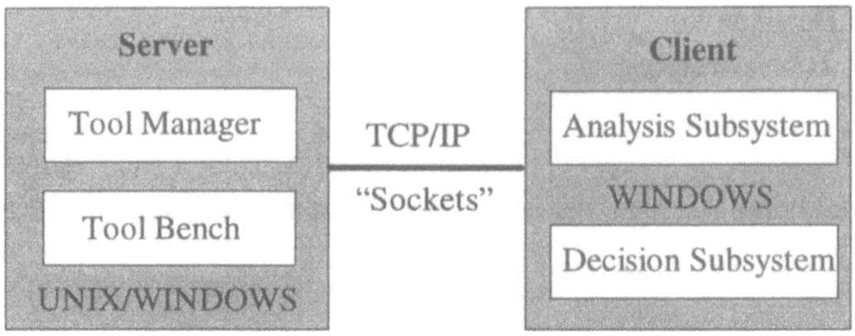

4.3 Mechanisms for Modularity

The architectural designs that were presented in the previous sections come together through several mechanisms (Application Programming Interfaces - API's, common data exchange formats, shared information and database schemes) by which the several modules of Orchestra interact to produce the integrated functionality that is envisaged. This section identifies the fundamental interface mechanisms that help to understand the "glue" of the Orchestra environment

All the actual API and other interfacing specifications are gathered in the project reports (available upon request). In this section we only mention their purpose and actual use.

4.3.1 Secure and Remote Archive API

The Orchestra/ELENIX 3.0 Secure and Remote Archive API allows the use of remote secure archives. These archives feature access control lists, concurrency control and dead archive.

4.3.2 Orchestra/Elenix 3.0 Document Generator API

The Orchestra/ELENIX 3.0 DG API allows the of the document generator module. This module is a lightweight application that assists on the production of documents.

4.3.3 Orchestra Workflow API - EWA (V1.00, Jul/96)

The ORCHESTRA/ELENIX 3.0 Workflow API is available to third party developers that wish to operate with the underlying data repository. This precise API is used to interact with the variables and graphic description files associated with flows and processes.

4.3.4 Orchestra/Elenix 3.0 Mail Api - ESMA (V2.00, Jun/96)

The Orchestra/Elenix 3.0 Simple Mail API provides direct access to the Elnix Mail services. It has been used in conjunction with the Contextual Communication modules and with the Negotiation and Decision subsystem.

5. Technical Information on Components and Prototypes

This chapter provides additional information on technical aspects of several Orchestra components, as well as short descriptions of some of the prototypes and experiments that were carried out in the scope of the project. It is meant to answer questions like "How was this component implemented ?", "Give me an example of the use of this component", or "What do I need to run this component ?". As such, the chapter is more a repository of technical information that can interest more curious readers.

5.1 Taskon/OORAM[34] technical data

TASKON/OORAM provides an environment for object-oriented analysis, design and implementation in areas such as enterprise modeling, information management systems, user interfaces, real time systems and telecommunication systems {Reenskaug et al.}. TASKON/OORAM is based on a pure object-oriented concept. Role models are the central construct. A role model describes how objects collaborate in a structure in order to perform some function of the overall system.

In role models, objects are like clerks in an organisation: They are organised in a structure of collaboration, where each clerk or object has its own responsibility within the organisation. A clerk has a *position* in the organisation, an object plays one or more *roles* in the structure of objects. A clerk has a certain *competence* which makes him qualified to fill one or more positions, an object has a *type* that gives it the behaviour it needs to play one or more roles. The task of the organizational consultant is to create an *effective work organisation*, the task of the

[34] Contact Taskon (see address in appendix)

system designer is to create an *effective role model* that organises the system's objects in an effective way.

In another analogy one may think of a role model as a certain act in a play. The actors collaborate in a certain structure to perform properly. The identity of the actor is not important as long as he/she fulfils the specific requirements of the role.

A role model may be observed in different perspectives. We may observe the system of interacting roles from different observation points. OORAM supports three points of observation, called ***perspectives:***

- *Environment perspective,* where the observer is placed in the system environment so that she can observe the system's interaction with its environment roles.
- *Inter role perspective,* where the observer is placed between the roles so that she can observe the messages flowing between them and indirectly deduce the role attributes.
- *Internal perspective*, where the observer is placed inside a role so that she can observe its implementation.

OORAM advantages:

- Role models describe object patterns.
- One model - many views
- Separation of concern
- Reuse through model inheritance
- Seamless bridge to implementation
- Easily customised to the business area

Different views in OORAM

Systems of interacting objects may be studied in different views, each view expressing certain aspects of the system of roles while suppressing others. OORAM analysis supports 7 views on the role model:

1. ***Application Organiser,*** gives the user the possibility to separate OORAM models into packages and modules.
2. ***Area Of Concern view***, which is a textual description of the phenomenon modelled by the role model.
3. ***Relation view***, showing how we attach meaning to the roles and the relationships between them.
4. ***Collaboration view***, showing the pattern of roles and the message paths between them.
5. ***Scenario View,*** showing example time sequences of messages flowing between the roles.

6. ***State Diagram view***. There may be one state diagram for each role. It describes the possible states of the role, the signals that are acceptable in each state, the action taken as a result of each signal, and the next state attained after the action is completed. The only kind of signal possible in our object model is the receipt of a message.
7. ***Method Specification View***. This view describes the messages to be sent from a method and its receiving roles.

The analyst can only observe views of the underlying model. When thinking about some interesting phenomenon, the OORAM analyst creates an object model of the phenomenon in her head. This model can only be captured on paper or a computer screen as one or more *views*, these views are different presentations of an underlying *manifest model*. In the case of a paper report, the underlying model is abstract in the sense that it has no explicit representation. In the case of a computer based system, the underlying model is represented in an object data base.

5.1.1 Hardware and operating systems

Window system: X-Windows, Microsoft Windows 3.1x/95/NT
Operating system: HPUX, SUN OS, AIX, Windows (MS-DOS).
Network: LAN Manager, TCP/IP, PCTCP, PCNFS, Novel.

5.1.2 Version/Date

Version 4.0 - October 1996

5.1.3 Language

English, Norwegian

5.1.4 Training

Courses	Length	Nr of trainees per trainer
Introduction to Object Orientation	1 day	
OORAM method and tools	3 days	6
Customised cources in OORAM	3-5 days	6

5.2 Orchestra/ELENIX Multimedia 3.0[35]

Description and Product details: ELENIX Multimedia 3.0. ELENIX Multimedia is an integrated office management system, offering a desktop simulating the real office environment, that integrates the organization's existing hardware, operating systems and office applications. From the set of its features, we highlight the following ones:

Client-Server architecture;

Multi-lingual user work environment in PCs, with MS-Windows user interface;

ELENIX Servers available for UNIX and Windows NT, offering several services that can be shared among ELENIX Multimedia users;

Data repository supported by bundled ORACLE® or INGRES® rdbms runtimes;
Work environment offering:

Configurable Electronic Document Archive, supporting transparent optical and magnetic disk storage of multimedia documents. The document archive has advanced security features[36] (ACLs, integrity control), concurrence control, version control and dead archive management.

Workflow service allowing for the implementation of complex organizational procedures. Some of the implemented features are :

- Graphic definition of organizational flows;
- Definition of stages and tasks (mandatory or optional).
- Definition of groups/roles of users
- Definition of variables associated with flows;
- Definition of conditional statements;
- Delegation with or without knowledge;
- Temporary suspension of processes;
- API for use with third-party form tools;
- Advanced access policy to variables, flows and processes;
- Alarms;
- Exportation of process data;

Electronic Mail and Fax, enabling the user to send and receive multimedia documents, stored in the Electronic Archive, directly from his/her desktop. The Electronic Mail supports discussion groups and multiple shared folders;

[35] Contact SMD Informática (see address in appendix)
[36] to be shipped in early 1997

Agenda, enabling the user to manage his/her personal appointments and schedule meetings involving several other users; this service also helps the management of the organization's resources (meeting rooms, presentations' material, company vehicles, etc.);

Document Indexing and Search, for fast search and retrieval of documents stored in the Electronic Archive; using this service, any document search can be done by author, title, subject, date, etc.;

Addresses Database Service, for storage and fast retrieval of address cards, used to keep information concerning people or organizations (names, addresses, phone and fax numbers, or other data);

Correspondence Log, for storing information about incoming or outgoing correspondence, and following its circulation within the organization;

Full text document retrieval and powerful cross query mechanisms on the data stored in ELENIX Multimedia based on BRS/SEARCH® package;

Disconnected mode operation for the Electronic Mail and Agenda services;
High level of integration among the services.

Run-time platforms

- Client operating system : MSWindows 3.1, Windows for Workgroups, Windows 95
- Server platforms and OS : UNIX (SCO UNIX, HP UX, IBM AIX, SunOS 4.1.x, Solaris 2.x, UNIX SysV 3.2,UNIX SVR4, DEC Ultrix, BULL - AIX compatible, ICL RISC 6000, SINIX), Windows NT
- Data repository : ORACLE, INGRES and INFORMIX rdbms.
- Network support : TCP/IP
- Price (average in ECU) : Client 359, Client with workflow 487, Server 1000

5.3 Information Systems Integration

The requirements of the ORCHESTRA pilot sites has been studied for contributing to the integration of ORCHESTRA system within the present corporate applications. The ENTIRE products have been installed and customized in each pilot, and also tested by writing small tailor-made programs. The examples that have been prepared to demonstrate this functionally are the following:

1. Access to a database located in a remote mainframe

2. Download data stored in VSAM files located in a mainframe, and subsequent report generation based on the ORCHESTRA Document Generator module
3. Transparent access to different database using the Fast Query tool.

The functionality of the Global Information system has been also profited for the interconnection between different ORCHESTRA modules; specially at the Contextual Communication Filter.

In Iberdrola-CONUC pilot, there was a ADABAS database located at a SCO-UNIX server with information of a nuclear power plant. This information refers to the nucleus of the reactor : its structure, the cycles, different types of combustible elements, suppliers, amount of consumed materials, statistics, and so on. A simple tailor-made application at the PC-Windows is the proper access to the database information. Two different ways of access have been tested:

- Remote access to the database : The user application at the PC-Windows accesses directly the remote database using NET-WORK to solve the database location problem, and ACCESS to solve the DBMS access/query problem. This approach is oriented to developers of custom applications. Programs are easy to implement and the data access is transparent to developer. But, the time response is usually slower since the network traffic.

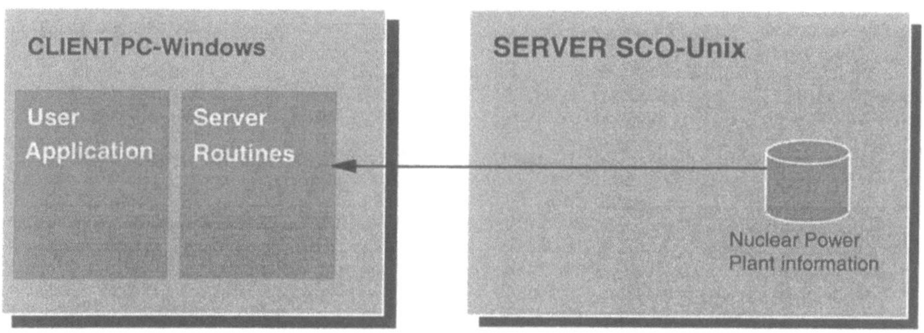

- Remote Procedure Call to routines that access the database locally : In this solution, BROKER manages the Client-Server communication. It provides several possible communication strategies: messaging, remote procedure call and conversational. Applications using these approaches are more complicated to develop because they do not only need of client modules, but also require the design and encapsulation of server modules. The advantages provided by these strategies are usually a faster program execution and a lower network usage.

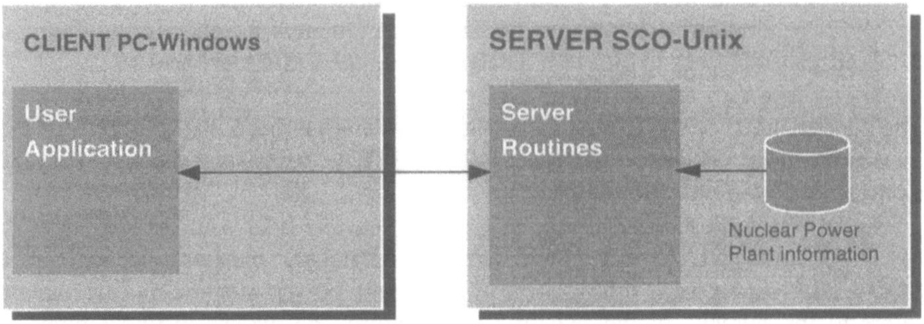

At EDINFOR-EDP pilot, the Global Information system has been used for the integration between a VSAM file located in a mainframe under MVS and the ORCHESTRA Document Generator utility. A tailor-made application generates a report with data from a VSAM file. Some relevant data stored the file are download to a PC file in a format readable for the Document Generator. Subsequently, the Document Generator makes up a report with this data. This application uses the ENTIRE-NETWORK functionality for the interrelation of client and server. The client module requires from the server routines for the data stored in the VSAM file.

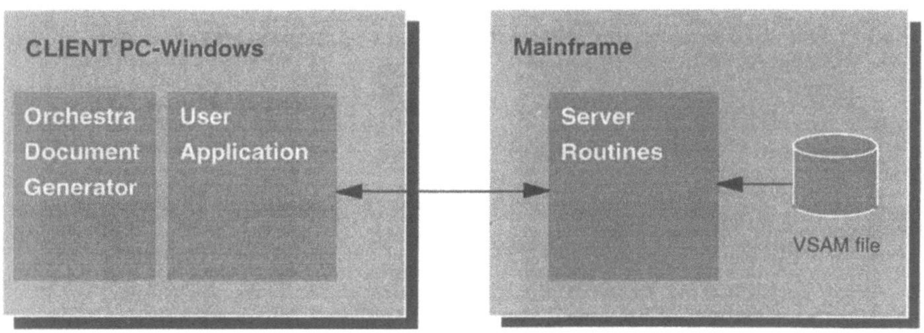

Fast Query and Legacy Databases. Different corporate databases in the ORCHESTRA project pilots have been analyzed in order to be accessed by the final users using the Fast Query tool. Their conceptual data models have been introduced on the Fast Query internal structure.

The Iberdrola-CONUC pilot possesses an ADABAS database in a UNIX machine. This database contains information about one nuclear power plant. Its conceptual data model is displayed on the next figure. This model represent nine database entities and facilities the access to many entity attributes (more than 75 fields).

Inside this framework, Fast Query can answer to requests, such as:
- Which are the suppliers of the combustible elements involved on the cycle nr. 6 ?
- How many types of combustible elements have been used once ?
- Which elements have been in the pool in the cycle with number 5 ?
- Which elements have consumed more than 500.000 units during the cycle 1 ?
- Which are the positions where there is no combustible element during the cycle 9 ?
- How many elements have been placed in more than two different positions ?
- Which places the combustible element with code XXX have been sited ?

The NATURAL query programs which have been generated by the Fast Query tool have been integrated in new tailor-made application for subsequent execution.

Figure 5-1. Conceptual model of the nuclear power plant database

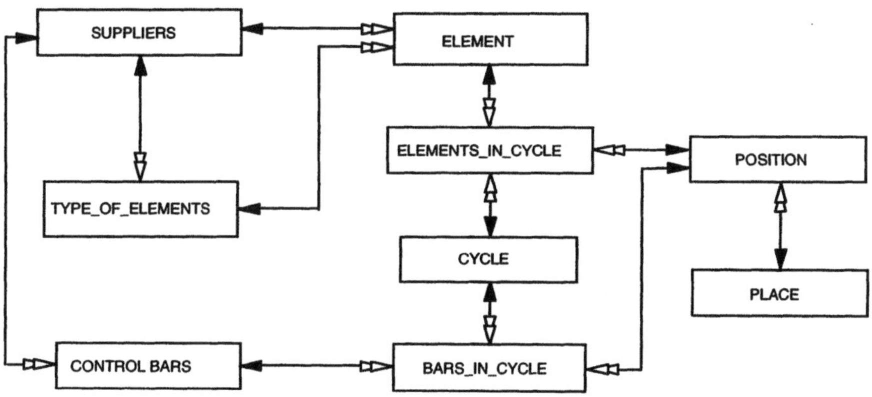

The EDINFOR-SINES pilot at Oporto (Portugal) owns a water commercial management system. This system contains a database which conceptual model is presented on the next figure. Nine of the database entities and more than one hundred of its fields are accessible from the Fast Query tool.

In this case, the tool provides a way to define query which answer questions like:
- Which client with code XXX is customer of the company 9999 ?
- Which rate is applied to the client sited on the site number Y ?
- Which are the diameters of the counters installed on the sites of the client XXX ?
- How many counters are installed with diameter equal 15 ?
- Which clients belong to the area X ?
- Which is the paying situation for the account of the client X ?
- How many service order have been generated by the client XXX ?
- Which are the counter readings of client XXX during the last two years?

At SINES pilot, the output of the Fast Query tool have been integrated with the ORCHESTRA Document Generator. Several reports are periodically generated by the Document Generator and the necessary data are obtained by executing the programs created with Fast Query.

Figure 5-2. Conceptual model of the SINES Water Commercial Management database

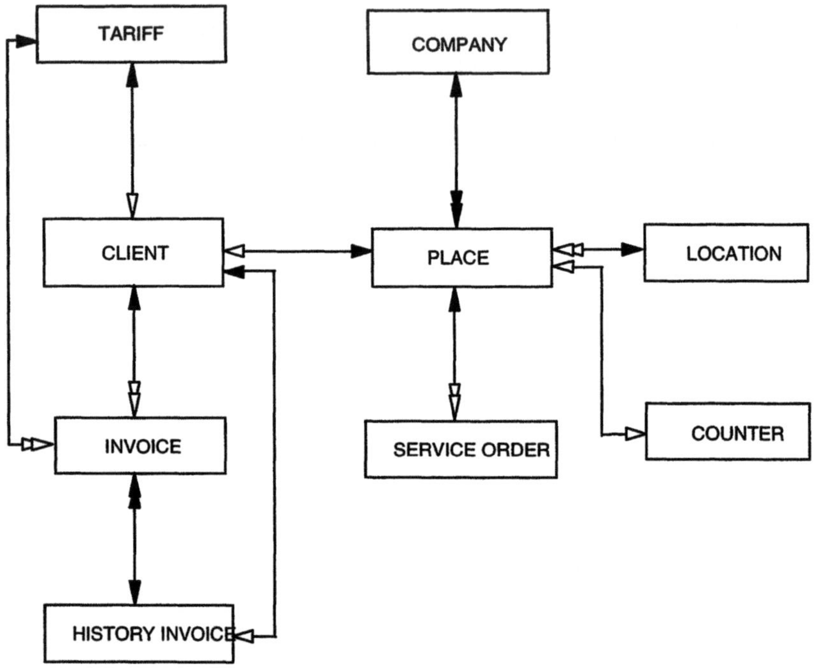

5.4 Contextual Communication

The Contextual Communication modules are depicted in next figure, integrated within the Orchestra environment. The specific modules belonging to the Contextual Communication are colored in dark gray.

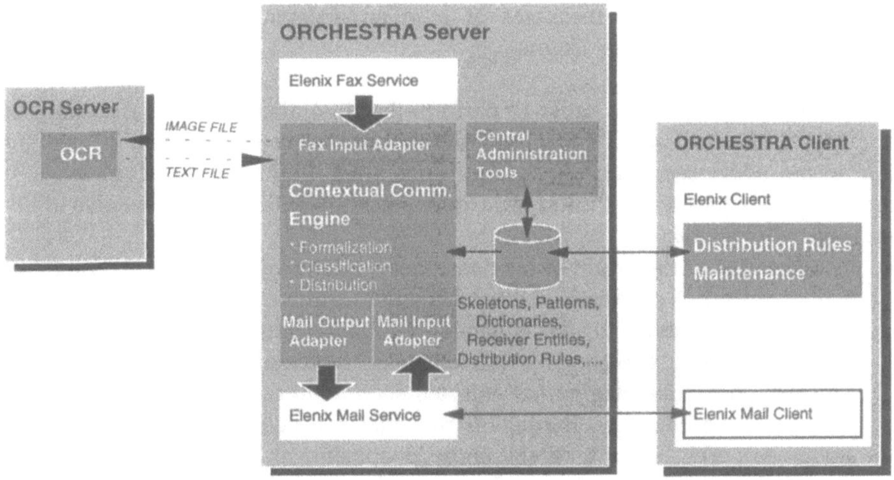

Figure 5-3 - Contextual Communication architecture as tested in the Pilots

Fax Input Adapter. The major information source used by the Contextual Communication at the Orchestra pilot organization has been the Fax service. A specific Fax Input Adapter has been developed in order to attach the Elenix Fax Service to the Contextual Communication Engine. The main topics addressed here have been:

- Automatic activation of the process when a fax document arrives: The Elenix Server allows the definition of a script to be executed when a fax arrives. This has been used by the Contextual Communication to activate the whole process.
- Conversion to electronic text format: A specific OCR Server process has been developed and integrated with the Contextual Communication. The OCR engine used has been *Calera* ®, from Calera Recognition Systems Inc, installed on a Windows platform. The communication between the OCR Server and the Contextual Communication Engine uses *Entire Broker*, from Software AG. The OCR Server converts the first page of the image received into an ASCII text file, that can be directly analyzed by the Contextual Engine.

Mail Input Adapter. Another information source that has been used by the Contextual Communication is the mail service. In this case, the purpose is the attachment to one or more common mailboxes (organizational or departmental), that are usually settled in the organizations. The Contextual Communication will then analyze the miscellaneous types of messages received, and automatically forward them to the proper persons. In order to get this attachment, the Elenix Mail Service has been integrated with the Contextual Communication. A tailored process checks for new messages at a given account, and obtained text is forwarded to the Contextual Engine.

Mail Output Adapter. In order to perform the final distribution of the analyzed documents, the mail service has been selected as the major distribution medium. For every addressee selected by the Contextual Engine, a mail message is produced on behalf of the Contextual Communication Service. The contents of this message will include:

- Identification of the origin of the document (in this case, a fax transmission or a mail message); A summary of the information extracted about the sender of the document; A summary of the semantic information extracted (subject explicitly quoted, semantic categories extracted, main keywords); The explanation of why the Contextual Engine has selected such addressee (document addressed to him or the specific distribution rule that caused the inclusion of a new addressee); The location of the entire document, or an attachment with the document (depending on the defined defaults, or the preferences stated in the distribution rules).

Again, the Elenix Mail Service has been used, in integration with the Contextual Communication, in order to produce the output messages to the selected addressees.

Contextual Communication Engine. The Contextual Communication Engine holds the core process of the Contextual Communication Services. It is settled as a server process running on the background at the Orchestra Server and waiting for process requests. The Engine has been developed in *Natural* (Software AG 4th.generation programming language) and C/C++. The interaction with the Server Process is managed by *Entire Broker*, which allows to transparently accept requests originated from remote clients as well as from local processes.

5.5 Management & Executive Information Systems

The Orchestra WF-MEIS Tool has been developed using the Taskon/Integrator. The approach followed by the Taskon/Integrator separates logically the modules of an Integrator Application into four classes:

- The Path module: Specifies the connections between the existing conceptual entities covered by the application, defines the available options for every one, and specifies the overall look-and-feel.
- The Report module: Includes every defined report (scope, format,...) which can be selected once a given conceptual entity has been selected.
- The Update module: Defines data update functions to be linked to the application.
- The Data module: Specifies the data structures (tables, formats, access infrastructure, physical location of the data sources) and all the low-level data functions (SQL queries).

The Orchestra WF-MEIS Tool has made use of the Path, Report and Data functions. Since the purpose of this tool in Orchestra was not to introduce modifications on the Workflow Database, the Update functions has not been used.

Path links. The Path module devised for the Orchestra WF-MEIS Tool covers all the major entities addressed on the Elenix Workflow data structure. These entities are depicted in the next figure, in which the path connections have also been specified.

Figure 5-4. Path links schema for WF-MEIS Tool

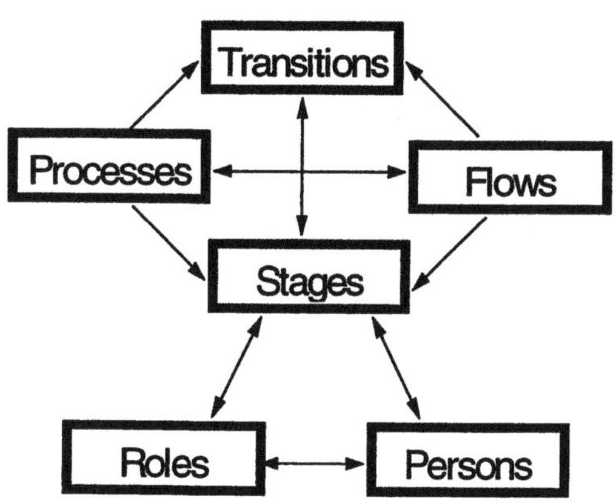

Reports. Once a given entity is selected, and a member of that entity has been highlighted, the WF-MEIS Tool allows to run a set of reports that has been defined for every one of the entities. The following is the complete list of the reports devised for the Workflow entities, and the General Reports, which are not allocated to a specific entity.

General Reports

- General Statistics; Per-flow Statistics; Get all delayed processes; Get all processes delayed more than a given time amount.

Persons

- Get person attributes, which roles he fills and which roles he might fill; Get pending processes; Get all finished processes; Get pending stages; Get all finished stages; Get all remaining stages in pending processes; Get all delayed processes; Get all processes delayed more than a given time amount; Get all delayed stages; Get all stages delayed more than a given time amount

Roles

- Get Role attributes, persons filling this role and persons who might fill it; Get stages and their processes; Get pending processes; Get all finished processes; Get pending stages; Get all finished stages; Get all remaining stages in pending processes; Get all delayed processes; Get all processes delayed more than a given time amount; Get all delayed stages; Get all stages delayed more than a given time amount.

Flows

- Get Flow attributes; Get stages, transitions, actions and conditions; Get roles involved, persons able to fulfill them and persons currently filling them; Average time to finish a process; Average number of persons involved in a flow; Get pending processes; Get all finished processes; Get pending stages; Get all finished stages; Get all remaining stages in pending processes; Get all delayed processes; Get all processes delayed more than a given time amount; Get all delayed stages; Get all stages delayed more than a given time amount

Processes

- Get Process attributes; Get stages, transitions, actions and conditions; Get roles involved, persons able to fulfill them and persons currently filling them; Get pending stages; Get all finished stages; Get all delayed stages; Get all stages delayed more than a given time amount

Stages

- Get Stage attributes; Get all involved actions and their attributes; Get roles involved, persons able to fulfill them and persons currently filling them; Get Transitions in and out the selected stage
- Transitions
- Get Transition attributes; Get all involved conditions and their attributes; Get Stages to and from the selected transition

Queries. Finally, the set of SQL queries that the rest of the modules can issue to retrieve database information are collected into the Data module, together with the database structure. The list of the queries defined for the WF-MEIS Tool comprise about 60 different queries, which can be used between each other. Those queries can be divided into two logical groups:

- Path choice queries
- Report queries

5.5.1 TASKON/Integrator Technical information

1. User interface: Window-based, graphical. May use multiple windows.
2. Technology platform:
   Window system: X-Windows, Microsoft Windows.
   Operating system: HPUX, SUN OS, Solaris, MS Windows 3.x/95/NT, OS/2
   Network: LAN Manager, TCP/IP, PCTCP, PCNFS, Novell.
   Databases: Standard relational database systems with SQL interface.
   No TASKON/Integrator software is running on the server. The following database systems are available:
     - Sybase
     - Oracle
     - DB2 via gateway
     - Microsoft ODBC

   Client requirements:
     - PC: Minimum 486/33 MHz
     - Minimum 16 Mbyte RAM for end-users, minimum 16 Mbyte RAM for developers
     - The software requires 15 Mbyte disk space

   Server hardware requirements: Depends on the database used.
3. Programming language: TASKON/Integrator is developed in Smalltalk using the VisualWorks product from ParcPlace-Digitalk, Inc.
4. User environment and application language: The user environment is available in English. A separate translation file is used to adapt applications to other languages. A Norwegian translation file is available.
5. Import/export:
   - The following file formats are supported: ASCII, CSV, RTF, SYLK.
   - Graphics and pictures: Copying of graphics and picture (bitmap format) is possible from any tool. On MS Windows, graphics is included in RTF files in meta-file format.
   - Support for OLE(1) and DDE access to MS Windows tools.
6. Print options: Postscript, black/white and color or via external tools.
7. Single-user/multiuser/network:
   The TASKON/Integrator is available in single-user, multiuser and network versions. In a network, the program can be installed on the

server, with the users working against the server, or the users can do computer-intensive transactions locally and access the server for requests and updates only.

Registered trademarks:
Windows, MS-DOS, ODBC and LAN Manager from Microsoft Corporation.
Sybase from Sybase, Inc. Oracle from Oracle Corporation, Inc.
DB2 from International Business Machines.
X-Windows from M.I.T. HPUX from Hewlett-Packard Company.
SUN OS, Solaris and PCNFS from Sun Microsystems.
Novell NetWare from Novell, Inc. PCTCP from FTP Software.
VisualWorks from ParcPlace-Digitalk, Inc.

5.6 Interactive Negotiation Tools

The main characteristics of the Negotiation system prototype, as presented in the final version of Orchestra, are:

- The Negotiation System is activated by an icon within the ORCHESTRA group of programmes and provides a direct access to the Analysis Subsystem. Once the Analysis Subsystem has generated a recommendation, instructions are sent to the Tool Manager. The Tool Manager manages the activation order to the Decision Subsystem.
- The Analysis Subsystem rests on the application of a Integrated Contingency Model (based on Vroom, Stumpf & Thompson models), being finally selected the numerical Vroom Model, suggested by the author himself.
- The Tool Bench includes a suite of tools that support different decision techniques: Brainstorming, Voting, Nominal Group Technique.

5.6.1 Prototype System Configuration

- PC 386 or above with 4 Mb of RAM and at least 10 Mb of disk space.
- Environment MS-Windows 3.x or posterior.
- Communications protocol TCP/IP compatible with WINSOCK.
- Platform for ELENIX Work Group 2.0 or superior

Analysis Subsystem Module

- Developed in Delphi 1.0
- Connected with the Tool Manager through "sockets"
- Located on the PC/Windows client

Decision Subsystem Module

- Developed in Visual C++
- Connected with the Tool Manager through M-Bus located on the PC/Windows client

Tool Manager

- Developed in Visual C++
- Located on the PC/SCO or UNIX Server

Tool Bench

- Developed in Visual C++
- Integrated into the Tool Manager
- Runs on Windows'95 (Communication server on Unix or Windows'95)

6. The Pilot Sites

The objectives of the introduction of pilot sites in the Orchestra project were twofold:

- To have a set of comprehensive case studies where organizational analysis and modeling could be performed. These case studies, and the specific characteristics and needs of each organization should also provide relevant information to support design decisions in the several Orchestra subsystems.
- To have a minimal set of end-users potentially interested to use the developments of the project, to be installed on a need basis at the users location.

This chapter summarizes the most interesting aspects of each one of the Orchestra pilots (drawn from the analysis performed according to the methodology described in chapter 2), what has actually happened in those pilots, and the contributions that were made by each one, and to each one of them by the remainder of the consortium. The final section presents a critical perspective on the experience gained in the relation between the pilots and the project as a whole.

6.1 EDP

6.1.1 From the Generic Analysis

This subsection mentions some aspects not referred to in previous sections but helpful to a better understanding of the EDP pilot. Edinfor has been as technical pilot, i.e. a testbed for some of the prototypes and technical experiences in the project. Therefore, Edinfor was not subject to the organizational analysis. Details like the organizational charts are available in the appropriate reports.

Formal Aspects	
Goals	Purpose - Production and distribution of energy Global Objective - minimize number of shots at the lowest cost. Specific Objectives according to the functional areas of the CTS. • Conduction - assure the work of the CTS's four groups of energy production. • Maintenance - support the conduction teams, in what concerns maintenance and repairing (electric and mechanic). • Administrative - to support the circulation of information from the interior to the exterior and vice-versa, personnel management, bookkeeping and budget control, cashier's operations, transport management of both workers and stocks, steward management, stocks management and purchasing.
Strategies	The prevailing conditions in the context of this organization seem to be stable[37] as we are dealing with a public company that controls (through a holding company) all the production and distribution of energy throughout the country. Bearing in mind what we defined earlier as the CTS's involving context and according to the typology of Miles and Snow (1986), this organization is close to the "Defensive" strategy, in which the effort for the reduction of production and distribution costs is the only alternative for rentability.
Formal Structure	CTS, involving around 200 people, directly depends on EDP Portugal, the Head Office of which is in Lisbon. According to the organization charts, there exist two top Heads and four staff organs (Secretary, GSCS, Environment and Chemistry and Technical Archive). The second Head supervises the Heads of the three big departments: Conduction, Maintenance and Administrative. • Conduction - This department has a Department Head, two staff units (Statistics and Exploration Analyses) and an Operational Head that co-ordinates five (5) GCI (internal conduction teams), each having a Team Head supervising four (4) Conduction Managers that guarantee the supervision of the 10 production Technical Operators and also of the 4 installation and ashes extraction Controllers. This department works through a command chain. • Maintenance - This department has a Department Head, a staff Organ (Programming) and two operational areas, the mechanical maintenance and the electrical maintenance, each

[37] During the execution of ORCHESTRA EDP was split into a number of companies with regional scope, thus changing some of the dependencies mentioned in this analysis.

	having a Team Head. Both areas have a support unit (Methods) and are divided into two sub-areas: Mechanic/Boilery, Electric/Control, each having a Team Chief and specialized workers. Their coordination is done by its Department Heads, i.e., by the hierarchy, with the support of the staff organ (Programming). There are formal procedures that regulate the interventions of each of the areas, and which obey to Pert networks and Gantt Charts. • Administrative - This department has a Department Head, who is in the same hierarchical level as the heads of the two other departments described above. He/she supervises a staff area (provisions) and seven functional areas (steward and transports, bureau, treasury, bookkeeping and budget, personnel, storehouse and purchasing), involving 19 people. Due to its attributions, this department develops a network of relationships with all the areas of the CTS.
Administrative Policies and Procedures	The Administrative Department maintains a procedures manual, conceived by the respective areas, used whenever necessary. It discriminates the way services should be provided and the forms needed to develop the work.
Administrative Systems	As the CTS directly depends on Lisboa, we cannot find specific economic and financial indicators for this Central. The Administrative Department only gives a set of inputs that allow EDP to construct build global indicators. The personnel management is ensured by the Personnel area of CTS (except for the wages processing).
Formal Reward Systems	In the pilot department, the performance objectives relate directly to the duties of the different areas. The objective is to perform its activities within a certain time period.

Social Factors	
Culture	The analyses of CTS's culture was made following the ethnographic method, recurring to the interviewees exposition of their own experience within the organization. The following aspects permit to highlight some cultural components that seem of interest: • The personnel is always ready to solve the problems that may affect the Central's effectiveness and efficiency; • Whenever necessary, workers join efforts and make known the obtained results, in order to compare them to the ones of other organizations of the group. Nevertheless, constructive collaboration is valued. • Everyone is involved in the improvement of production processes, in order to increase the quality indexes.

	• There are functional mismatches among departments, with special emphasis for the administrative department. • Formality is present both in inter-departments relationships and within-departments relationships. • The CTS's effectiveness is supported by competitive values relatively to the similar organizations of the group, which justifies the motivation for problem solving, when performance is at risk. Values associated with the working process: • Security - Given the characteristics of this type of organization (permanent contact with electric and mechanical components), the proliferation of advise to guarantee this value is understandable: informative posters, formal documents exchanged between different areas, obedience to security legislation and its control. • Specialization versus autonomy - Autonomy in decision making does not stand by the strong technical specialization and responsibility of most of the workers. One of the desirable values is, precisely, to reduce this gap through an increase in autonomy. • Bureaucracy (in the organizational theory sense) - work is organized in routine processes with a number of written procedures and several authorization levels. • Resistance to change - In the basis of the structure we feel resistance to computerization and elimination of procedures considered to be redundant. According to Quinn (1988) we are dealing here with a culture that is centered in internal procedures, with some capacity to respond to dynamic and unstable involving environments through innovation. Normalization and control are the favorite means to achieve the organizations objectives. The Head of the pilot department delegates responsibilities, but there is no autonomy for decision making in the respective areas: any formal document must be signed by the direct chief.
Interaction Processes, Networks and Social Patterns	The more frequent interactions are interpersonal relationships, although formal. Information about work follows the defined command chain and are supported by internal communications and circular letters. To solve restrict and/or sporadic problems that involve a certain risk, the people in charge for the different areas organize meetings in order to accelerate problem solving.
Individual Attributes	In a general manner the elements of the pilot department and of the other two departments perceive the CTS as a prestigious organization, with good performances within EDP. This leads to a

	high sense of ownership among the workers of the different hierarchical levels.

Technology	
Tools, equipment and machinery	The support of the work is done by a computer controlled technologic equipment with a high degree of complexity. Energy production is controlled by a command room, that can give, at any moment, a wide range of indicators and that requires high levels of vigilance and technical competence from its operators. Manual tools are used in the maintenance of the equipment for the production of energy. The Administrative Department uses PC based personal productivity tools.
Job Design	The analysis only focused on the Administrative Department, as is determined by the existing limitations on the diagnoses of the pilot. In this department, jobs are organized in such a way that it becomes possible to respond to the seven functions described above. The jobs are, in general, routine tasks. The necessity of working with specific computer tools requests quite concrete competencies that have to be developed and updated.
Work Design	(see deliverables and OORAM models)
Technical expertise	The type of work undertaken in the administrative Department requests some skills in the respective areas but does not require a high degree of specialization nor university education. Procedures are normalized to such an extent that makes it difficult for the workers to comprehend and accept new ways of working. Many workers have problems in using computers.
Technical policies and procedures	Regarding the areas that directly relate to energy production and maintenance, there are technical procedures used as guidelines for the work, planned and defined by Programming and Methods. For the Administrative area, the procedures manual describes attributions, working methods, and forms that must be used for each attribution.
Technical systems	The existence, in the Administrative Department, of control and provision systems, namely for the storehouse and purchasing, deserves being highlighted. These systems were mentioned above, but we must add that they are not optimal: there are some failures, namely at the level of stocks management.

6.1.2 Fundamental Characteristics

EDP CTS, and its Administrative Department in particular as the pilot, had a set of fundamental characteristics that can be drawn from the analysis made above:

- An essentially operational organization, with well defined roles and systematic procedures, i.e., a good example of a strongly formalized organization, where the impact of an office platform equipped with a workflow functionality could be envisaged as of significant potential.
- An organization with real constraints concerning experimental activities, and therefore, as history showed later, a problematic ground for sociotechnical experiments, in spite of the openness and collaboration of the workers at CTS.
- An undefined environment concerning computing facilities, specially in what concerned the integration with EDP´s more general strategic decisions regarding adoption of groupware tools, electronic mail, etc..

6.1.3 Activities carried out in the pilot[38]

The participation of EDP and Edinfor in Orchestra was influenced by a number of critical aspects:

- The process of division of EDP into a number of smaller companies, and the preparation of its privatization.
- The dimension and complexity of the EDP structure and the need to leave the daily operation as much as possible undisturbed.
- The collaboration of Edinfor, the 2nd company of the EDP group, responsible - for the operation and management of the Data Processing Centers, computing systems, applications, communications, for all the companies/units of the group.

These conditions led to the choice of the Thermal Powerplant of Sines for Orchestra, a unit of EDP, together with Edinfor. Concerning Edinfor, its participation was also motivated by other factors, directly related with the project's objectives:

- The participation in an European project including a large number of companies from several countries allows a better knowledge and harnessing of information technology problems and solutions, applicable to the business areas of the EDP group and Edinfor in particular.
- The nature of the technological goals of Orchestra, mainly in the areas of open systems architectures and integration, complemented the know-how of Edinfor (essentially directed towards mainframe-based solutions and platforms).
- The possibility of creating a laboratory with one of the units of the EDP group and to evaluate groupware solutions in context.
- The further exploitation of the SAG technology, already deployed in several EDP and Edinfor locations.

---

[38] As viewed by Carlos Raposo, from Edinfor, and summarized by the editor (nmg).

The development of the activities in the project had periods of different pace and work intensity, which can be divided in three essential phases:

1. The initial phase corresponding to the first 4 to 5 months of the project:
- Resolution of the administrative aspects of the project
- Deeper knowledge of the remaining partners in the consortium, discussion and planning
- Creation of the project's team at EDP-CTS and Edinfor, coordination, work planning, and control
- Links with the coordinators of other tasks in the project
- Installation of the Orchestra basic platform (Elenix), and SAG products.
2. This phase corresponds to the intermediate period of around 14 months, and was directed to the development of the work planned in the areas of Analysis of the pilots organizations, definition and analysis of the prototypes related with the Global Information System, efforts of application, integration and trial, and project management. In particular, it included:
- Acquisition and installation of generic equipment and software
- Installation of Elenix and SAG products
- Training of people from EDP-CTS in the Elenix environment
- Selection of workflows to be considered in the Orchestra/Elenix prototypes
- Selection of management information (extracted from VSAM files) for demonstration of mainframe access.
- Analysis of the feasibility of integrating CONNECT (mainframe based email) with the Elenix mail services and generic Internet mail.

During this phase, Edinfor assumed the role of pilot more clearly, serving as a testbed for the prototypes, prior to their deployment into EDP-CTS. In this context, the following activities were carried out:
- Replication of the hw/sw integration platforms at Edinfor and INESC
- Strong interaction and collaboration in the development and test of the Fast Query prototypes with SAG, together with the use and experimentation of the new Orchestra/Elenix Document Generation system.
- Participation in the construction of the Contextual Communication prototype, specially in what concerns configuration and integration of the system with the organizational information of Edinfor and EDP-CTS.
3. This phase corresponds to the final period (last six months) and relates with all the final efforts towards prototype integration
    - Revision of schedules for integration, demonstration and reporting
    - Participation in the intermediate reviews.
    - Contribution to the project final report[39].

[39] This particular section in this report.

6.2 Comunicações Nacionais

6.2.1 From the generic analysis

This subsection mentions some aspects not referred to in previous sections but helpful to a better understanding of the Comunicações Nacionais (CN) pilot. Details like the organizational charts are available in the appropriate reports.

Formal Aspects	
Goals	Purpose - Manage the State's participation in the Telecom & Postal Services Global Objective - Provide consultancy services to the Administration, regarding the making of decisions on the business areas and act as an observer in some processes. Specific Objectives - The Administrative Department Management (ADM) has, as its main objectives, the promotion of organizational and rationalization systems, the elaboration of the budget, and the exercise of the administrative functions. The Executive Back-up Staff (EBS) has to support, study and support CN's decisions, at the juridical, strategic, financial and software levels.
Strategies	CN's environment can be characterized by its weak demand explosion, its modernization and technologies improvement in the field of communications, in a context of progressive liberalization and privatization. The market's liberalization and privatization seems to be a threat to CN.[40] The bet in the innovation and modernization of the production systems and in the offer of new services in the area of telecommunications, has been the strategy used. According to the typology of Miles and Snow (1986) CN would be characterized, in strategic terms, as a "Prospector" in the telecommunications area, once it tends to use its capacities for the development of innovations in both technologies and products. In the Postal Services area, CN follows a "Defensive" strategy.
Formal Structure	CN's structure is not formalized in an organization chart. CN is a holding company managing 50 participations, organized around two important business areas: Telecommunications and Postal Services. The telecommunications sector is comprised of two large enterprises: Telecom Portugal and Marconi. Although there is no

[40] As mentioned before, CN was closed by a Government decision on September 1995, after the merge of the several Telecom operators into one common company, Portugal Telecom.

	organizational scheme as such of this company, there is an Administrative Board composed of seven members (four members belong to the Executive Committee while the remaining three are chair people of holdings (Postal Services, Marconi and Telecommunications), the Administrative department Management (ADM) and the Executive Back-up Staff (Consultant Workers). The ADM is placed under the direct supervision of the general Secretary (whose role is to offer the Board of Directors back-up and see that its orders, as well as the decisions made by the Executive Committee, are carried out) it is composed of four distinct areas: Accounts and Treasury, Filing, Personnel and General Services. The Executive Back-up Staff is directly dependent on the Executive Committee and works in four centers (Computer Center, Legal Center, Management and Financial CO-ordination and Strategic Planning Center). The functions of the several areas are described in detail in the appropriate report.
Administrative Policies and Procedures	Given the strategic character of the organization and the high technical specialization of each of the elements of this unit, the work they do does not have any support at the level of the way it is done. To a certain extent we find an exception at the ADM where we find more routine processes.
Administrative Systems	Being a holding, CN has a set of administrative systems that regulate the economic, financial, and personnel activity. Some of these systems are: Balance Sheets; Operating Accounts/Gains and Losses; Personnel structure; Treasury; Investment and installed capacity; Performance indexes values; Data on domestic markets and main external markets; Inventory of the agreements between the main competing foreign companies in the global Telecommunications market.
Formal Reward Systems	An organization such as this one does not have performance objectives formally defined. Its effective workers (at the EBS) have to respond, the faster they can, to the Administration's solicitations, which can vary considerably. Its evaluation is thus closely related to the capacity to respond and to the way of solving problems, and is undertaken by the administration itself.

Social factors	
Culture	Internally, CN seems to have two distinct cultural environments, corresponding to EBS and ADM. Within the former, values such as flexibility, mutual help, and availability, support informal relationships, in order to obtain global results. In fact, the type of work developed there, calls for multidisciplinarity, congregation of know-how, and collective discussion before decision making. At the ADM work is more structured and there is more routine work,

	which requests some technical specialization of the workers. Communication thus becomes more formal, following a well defined command network. It seems to us that the values underlying these relationships are authority and normalization. According to the Typology of Quinn (1988) for the case of EBS we would be facing a culture of open systems and rational objectives, where innovation and concern for the involving environment are fundamental for the adaptation to the demands of a continuously changing market. ADM would be classified as having a culture centered in internal proceedings and results, via the high value given to information management mechanisms.
Interaction Processes, Networks and Social Patterns	For almost all the decision processes the EBS workers need to consult each other in order to support their decisions in all their components. The information is transmitted in a report and than discussed orally. Interaction between two or more elements are frequent, to discuss and build up documents together. There is no formal planning of meetings when they happen between elements of the EBS.
Individual Attributes	In general, CN's workers consider it to be a prestigious organization that is fundamental for the Group's effectiveness, which is composed by some of the biggest domestic companies. This leads to a strong feeling of ownership among the workers of all hierarchical levels. The type of work done at CN, mainly at EBS, requests very specific individual characteristics, such as communication and interaction skills.

Technology	
Tools, equipment and machinery	Being a provider of services, CN's technology is based on its workers' know-how, and in the existing computer tools that are at the workers disposal for the execution of their tasks. At the hardware level, CN has 60 PCs and at the level of software it works with Windows, a program for the consolidation of accounts and accountancy (Computer Land), a program for stocks management and a program for salaries processing.
Job Design	Once more, we found out differences the organization of jobs between the two CN areas that we have been: EBS and ADM. For the first one jobs are organized by their specific competencies with a high degree of complexity and, most of the time, with decision making autonomy. In the ADM there are mainly routine tasks, which, in some cases request a few specialization. Workers in this area have very few autonomy, being to a great extent dependent on their hierarchical superior.

Work Design	(see OORAM models)
Technical expertise	Given the great complexity of the work undertaken at EBS, it is fundamental that its workers have a high individual technical expertise. This workers have a degree suited for the area in which they work (lawyers, economists, computer engineers, etc.). At the ADM there exists a wither variety of tasks, from security to the area's responsible. Tasks are mainly routine functions, being although necessary to have a specific expertise for each of them.
Technical policies and procedures	Except for the Hardware and software manuals, there are no written procedures that would define the way of working with the different existing equipment.
Technical systems	Work planning and co-ordination - The meetings we present in what follows have a periodic and formal character and are part of procedure of the work planning and co-ordination. The Executive Committee calls meetings 1 or 2 months in advance. The Administration Board meets, in average, once in every three weeks with the participated companies. CN's administration meets every week. The agenda is set by the President, as a result of an analyses of the agenda proposed by each of the administrators. The agenda, as well as all the documents that are necessary for the meeting, is handed out 1 or 2 days before the meeting. The General Secretary makes a report of each meeting which is written down in the book after being approved by the participants. Meetings within the ADM are very informal, involving only 2 to 3 people. Every time a meeting is needed to discuss any issue, people contact one another directly by phone. Within ADM and in its relations with other CN's departments, we can consider that there exists a more or less regular meeting organized in sub-meetings - the budget meeting. The entities that have a seat are: ADM's director and the heads of Accounts and Budgeting, Management and Financial Co-ordination, Strategic Planning and Computer Center. It is worth mentioning that now on CN will start functioning by cost centers.
Control systems	In the EBS, at the level of Management and Financial Co-ordination, there exist some formal procedures mainly for the relations with the ADM. In the other departments of this area and once we are dealing with highly specialized workers, we can talk about a system of self control, which does not request any formal procedures of external control.

6.2.2 Fundamental Characteristics

To the objectives of Orchestra, CN was a particular kind of companies, where the Decision aspects were expected to be a core issue, when compared with the more routine tasks of operational work. In fact, CN de-emphasized the relevance of work automation (through Workflow system support for example), and brought to the foreground the interest of Orchestra subsystems like EIS integration, Contextual Communication and Decision and Negotiation tools.

6.2.3 Activities carried out in the pilot

The CN pilot was, during the initial year of the project, a very promising pilot. This promises were justified by the following factors:

- A strong enthusiasm in the management and technical staff concerning the project's objectives and general area of work.
- The option for the Orchestra base technology (Elenix) as the core groupware system to be installed and used at CN, which made all the planning for further integration of Orchestra prototypes much easier.

After the acquisition and installation of the hardware and Elenix 2.0 system, CN went through a significant effort of configuring the system (for example, definition of Correspondence Log policies, Archive layout, users configuration, etc.), together with a two step process (July 1995) of training a significant number of persons to use the system in their daily activities (around 15 users).

In parallel with this effort of technology deployment, the organizational analysis was carried out as can be observed from the project's reports and deliverables. A significant effort was put in the demonstration that occurred in the project's second review (August 1995).

On September 1995, due to the fact that the 1st phase of Portugal Telecom privatization had been concluded, (after a merge of all the Telecom companies - participated by CN - into Portugal Telecom), the meaning of CN ceased to exist and the Portuguese Government closed the company. As a result, attempts were still made to find an alternative pilot, to where equipment, software and prototypes could be moved. The possibility of using Correios e Telecomunicações de Portugal (Postal Services) was raised and evaluated but, after some weeks of negotiation (between end of 1995, beginning of 1996) and feedback from the project's review committee obtained in the project's 3rd review (Madrid, February 1996), the conclusion that was reached considered that, four months before the end of the project's terminal date, it did not make sense to include a new pilot and go through all the analysis, configuration and demonstration process.

6.3 CONUC/UITESA

6.3.1 From the generic analysis

This subsection mentions some aspects not referred to in previous sections but helpful to a better understanding of the CONUC (Combustible Nuclear) pilot. Details like the organizational charts are available in the appropriate reports.

Formal Aspects	
Goals	Purpose - To continuously have a competitive power and energy offer, obtaining the maximum economic income, and to select and manage, among the possible options of electric energy, the one that meets more efficiently the demand. Global Objective - To provide a quality service, to continuously empower its human resources in order to give an impulse to technological development and to maintain the leadership in innovation, economic and social improvement, and in constant care for the environment. Specific Objectives - CONUC has as its main objective, the management of nuclear energy, in order to ensure the fulfillment of the demand of all the other participated power plants, through a wide range of options with the best security, quality, price and term conditions.
Strategies	According to the Typology of Milles and Snow (1986), this unit would be classified as "Defensive" in terms of its strategy, as it provides a stable and limited range of services, puts a great emphasis in costs, has a functional structure and a high degree of specialization of its workers; the decision making and control at the operational l(technical) level are each worker responsibility. Nevertheless, strategic decision making and control are centralized.
Formal Structure	CONUC comprehends seven operation sections and a bureau. The latter gives support to the unit chief and to all other units. Each of these sections has only one worker with a high degree of specialization in engineering or physics (except for the secretaries.The unit/pilot is composed of several parts: 1. Nuclear Analysis: Fuel lattices models developments; Core models evaluations; Nuclear methods application; Criticality safety analysis. 2. Thermalhydro Analysis: Reactor and plant models development; Operational transients analysis; Thermal-

	hydraulics methods applications; Licensing accident analysis 3. Secretary: Files control and management; Budgets and orders control; Staff administration; Fax, typing, mailing, etc... 4. Methods: Calculation methods evaluation; Licensing topical reports generation; Application procedures maintenance; Regulatory body technical staff relation ship. 5. Codes Administration: System administration; Codes and methods implementation; Operational support to users; Software application QC. 6. Developments: Process computer; Nuclear design tools; R+D programs; Operational support tools. 7. Engineering: Engineering contract administration; Reloads nuclear design; Core safety evaluation; Reloads licensing. 8. Projects: Operational support co-ordination; Exposure accounting; Fuel performance evaluation; Operational strategy analysis
Administrative Policies and Procedures	Given the high degree of technical specialization of each of the workers of this unit, the work they undertake does not have any supports regarding the way it should be performed. The Bureau is an exception as it has a support document called "Manual of the Organization" covering the whole organization in a general way, except for the essential procedures specific to the unit. We must mention that one of this unit's objectives is to have, until the end of the year, a procedures manual for each of the sections. Their elaboration is being undertaken by the elements of each section.
Administrative Systems	This unit has an annual budget, which has a sub-division for each of the sections. They have to manage their budget, being aloud to deviate by ±5%. There are no economic or financial ratios for this unit, neither any personnel management system or pre-defined information systems.
Formal Reward Systems	Nuclear Fuel (CONUC), has a set of pre-defined objectives, and an evaluation and performance reward scheme for the whole unit. The sections do not presently have any defined objectives (they are being prepared). Thus a performance evaluation and a reward system, of either a monetary or symbolic character, are not possible.

Social Factors	
Culture	Within CONUC, privilege is given to relationships supported by informality and values like flexibility and being always at the disposal of the unit in order to obtain global results. The high degree of specialization and specificity of each worker's know-how, leads to informal and immediate contacts between them, whenever they need to communicate with each other. The workers of this area

	are experts in nuclear fuel, leading to a feeling of ownership among them, even if each is a specialist only in its own area (which simultaneously generates a certain individualism). According to the typology of Quinn (1988) we are facing a culture that is centered in the internal procedures and in its results or rational objectives, via the valorization of information management mechanisms, that promote control and stability, and also via efficiency and prosecution of the final objectives. This is why a great importance is given to the development of procedures manuals (are being elaborated) and to objectives setting for each of CONUC's sections.
Interaction Processes, Networks and Social Patterns	Interpersonal contacts occur whenever the opinion of one section is needed on the work done by other section. The information circulates orally or in an informal document. This type of interactions is only possible due to the similar academic background (Engineers and Physicists) of the unit's elements, permitting quick contacts and immediate understanding. Formally, there is a meeting every two weeks, where all sections are present (its objective is the definition of each elements necessities and priority setting). When problems emerge from lack of communication they tend to be solved by the participants. The chief only sets priorities, defining who is working with whom, in a certain moment. Each section is responsible for the projects belonging to its attributions, recurring to the other sections if necessary. we can consider that there exists a set of small firms that consults the others whenever needed, but never dropping the responsibility for the realization of the task. If possible, doubts are always solved by consulting the other sections. If the doubt relates only to the own specialization, it will be solved recurring to the unit chief or to the exterior.
Individual Attributes	Generally speaking, CONUC's elements see it as a prestigious unit, fundamental for the efficacy of IBERDROLA, one of the biggest Spanish companies. This leads to a strong ownership feeling among the workers, although some individuals showed they were not satisfied. In this unit work a group of nuclear fuel experts, who have a high degree of responsibility and specialization, supported by deep technical knowledge. This leads to a certain individualism, being the communication some times difficult. The group permanently emphasizes the individuals' technical characteristics but never the social ones. This demonstrates the individualist attitude prevailing in the unit.

Technology	
Tools, equipment and machinery	Being an organization aimed at services provision, its technology is based on its workers' Know-how and on the existing computer tools that are at the workers disposal for the realization of their jobs
Job Design	Each unit, in the person of its chief, has a great autonomy. In what concerns to the sections, we can verify that, for all of them, there is a great autonomy.
Work Design	(see OORAM models)
Technical expertise	Given the high degree of complexity of the work realized in CONUC, it is fundamental that this unit workers have a great individual technical competence, which is reinforced by the work organization - each person is responsible/operator for one area. It is fundamental to have a university education and a specialization in nuclear power
Technical policies and procedures	The existing user's manuals for the equipment are seldom used. The workers learn how to use the equipment (software/hardware) by try and error or asking the colleagues (the development section plays a main role).
Technical systems	Since these workers have a high degree of specialization, we can talk about a self-control system, that does not request any formal procedures of external control.Every two weeks a meeting is called, aiming at informing about all the work going on and at proceeding to the necessary adjustments to make all the work compatible..

6.3.2 Fundamental Characteristics

CONUC, the pilot intermediated by UITESA, was, in a large sense, similar to CN, insofar it involved a small number of people, charged with highly specialized and technical work. The formalization of some procedures had, on the other hand, an interesting potential for rehearsal of the more automation-oriented functionalities of Orchestra

6.3.3 Activities carried out in the pilot

The activities carried out at CONUC, with a strong and successful effort from UITESA, were similar of the ones that happened in the other pilots:

- Organizational Analysis, with some delay with respect to the pilots located in Portugal, both for logistic and linguistic reasons,
- Installation of Orchestra base platform, Elenix, with some delay due to the refinement of the translation of the Elenix software to the Spanish language.

This translation was not done explicitly for Orchestra but, by coincidence, was being carried out in sync.

- Identification of possible work flows and configuration of the Orchestra prototypes considered relevant (Fast Query, Contextual Communication).
- Preparation of the project's 3rd Review, which took place in Madrid, on February 1st, 1996.

The final efforts relate with the definition of a plan for a further use and exploitation of Orchestra results, namely Orchestra/Elenix 3.0, the Fast Query tools, the Security functionality, and the Contextual Communication.

6.4 BEST

The BEST pilot was a (sub-)pilot or Orchestra, specially introduced to support Taskon activities in the project. This subsection presents a short description of BEST, in a structure that obviously differs from the previous ones.

Formal Aspects	
Goal	The Best program involves the most important companies in Norwegian industry and will contribute in the following areas: Co-operation among Norwegian industry, Exchange of knowledge and practical experience, Skills upgrading
Strategy	Exchange of experience on electronic co-operation and task processing amongst industry, research institutes and universities Initiate collaborative projects on electronic co-operation and/or task processing Implement, use, and refine a set of tools for co-operation in distributed organizations in SINTEF/NTH and demonstrate to industry Contribute to spreading the co-operation toolset to at least three companies Collect and enhance knowledge on development and implementation of task processing systems, and implement this into the curriculum at NTH Contribute to eleven PhD's within the BEST scope

Best partners

SINTEF/NTH	SINTEF is a non-profit R&D organization with a staff of about 2400 engaged in all aspects of contract research. It is closely associated with The Norwegian Institute of Technology (NTH) which is part of the University of Trondheim. A significant part of SINTEF's research activities is conducted on premises belonging to NTH, and personnel from both institutions often co-operate closely on the same projects. SINTEF and NTH have a total staff of approx. 500 engaged in Information Technology R&D. NTH has approx. 1200 Information Technology students in its M.Sc. programme, and is rapidly expanding its Ph.D. programme.
Statoil	Statoil is an oil company, founded in 1972, entirely owned by the Norwegian government. Its business covers investigation and recovery of oil and gas fields, transport and marketing of petroleum and related products as well as other types of business (e.g., petrol stations). The company had a turnover in 1993 on 81 billion Norwegian kroner (about 10 billion ECU). It has about 12000 employees. Statoil is the leading oil company on the Norwegian continental shelf, and is also the biggest marketing agent and distributor of petrol in Scandinavia.
Uni-Storebrand	Uni was founded in 1767 and merged with Storebrand in 1991. Today the concern is one of the 4 leading companies in Norway consisting of divisions for international insurance, administration of estates, and administration of loans. The total number of employees is 4100 and the result for 1994 was 253 million NOK.
Norsk Hydro	Norsk Hydro was founded in 1905 for the purpose of utilizing the resources of the Norwegian water falls to produce fertilizer based on nitrogen. Hydro is the leading producing company of fertilizer in Europe. By the end of 1994 the total number of employees was 32416. Total turnover in 1994 was NOK 71 billion (9 billion ECU) and the result was 7 billion. Oil and gas division represented 3 billion NOK, agriculture 1.5 billion NOK, aluminum 1.6, petro-chemical industry 0.9
Saga	Saga Petroleum was founded in 1972 by private Norwegian investors who wished to participate in the country's oil industry. Total number of employees at year-end 1994 was 1 323. In 1994 Saga's operating profit was NOK 1.5 billion (about 0.2 billion ECU) Profit before taxes was NOK 1 211 million. Saga participated in 11 of the 21 exploration wells spudded on the Norwegian shelf in 1994. Saga is operator of the Snorre, Tordis and Vigdis fields, and is one of the world's leading operators of deepwater production facilities.
DnB	Den Norske Bank (DNB) is the leading banking concern in Norway. The bank was founded in 1990 by a mercer between Bergen Bank, founded in 1855, and Den norske Creditbank, founded in 1857. The group is the main bankconnection for the 300 leading firms in Norway.

	By the end of 1994 the total number of employees was 6148. The result in 1994 was 2.7 billion NOK
NOVIT	NOVIT AS is a vendor and executor of software for banks and financial institutions. It is both a software user (in-house developed and 3rd party software) and a software vendor (develops customized software systems). Its market share in Norway is 25%. NOVIT AS has 319 employees and 25% of these are involved with software production. The company is organized into 3 main organizational units (Trondheim, Bergen and Oslo) and 7 main activity areas (Management, Development and Integration, Implementation, Operation and Installation, Support, Marketing and Purchasing).

6.4.1 Activities carried out in the pilot

The activities carried out together with the BEST partners, guided by Taskon were centered on the use of preliminary test cases for the use of Taskon OORAM as a workflow modelling tool. The set of deliverables, and the significant amount of technical and experimental knowledge, that was described in the first sections of Chapter 3, the ones concerning modeling, could not have been attained without the existence of the BEST pilot. As such, the pilot provided a proof of concept of the use of the ORCHESTRA modeling approach in real cases.

7. Market and Exploitation

This chapter provides pointers to a dedicated set of reports that provide respectively an analysis of the Market for Orchestra, the definition of the product(s), and the exploitation of the project's results. For several reasons, among which confidentiality, no concrete data is provided here.

7.1 The Market for Orchestra

The first report on Marketing and Exploitation analyses the Market for Orchestra under a particular perspective, the one centered on the Workflow and Office products. Orchestra results being more than just Workflow and Office products, were however considered to be marketable in that Market segment and therefore all the reasoning was based on the analysis of that market.

7.2 Products and Services Definition

The second report identifies individual products derived from the several Orchestra Components, the main of them being the Orchestra/Elenix 3.0 (including Workflow capabilities), the results obtained in the Global Information System (i.e. Orchestra Fast Query) and the Orchestra Contextual Communication Server. An attempt is made to define a GLOBAL SERVICE of organizational analysis and selective automation. No feasibility analysis is made in what concerns the economical advantage of such service, at least until a framework of agreements between the several partners in the project can be created.

7.3 Direct Exploitation by Industrial Partners

The third part includes the exploitation plans of the partners, with particular emphasis on the industrial partners (SMD, SAG, Taskon and Novabase). An overall exploitation plan is designed and presented prospectively, based on a critical aggregation of the individual exploitation plans. This final contribution is being worked out at the moment of the release of this preliminary version of the Report (July 1996).

8. The Orchestra Partners

This section summarizes the nature of the Orchestra partners. The description allows for a better understanding of the partners capabilities and interests. Addresses and contact points are given in Appendix.

8.1 INESC

INESC - Instituto de Engenharia de Sistemas e Computadores (Institute for Systems and Computer Engineering) is a private, non-profit association, dedicated to research, technological development, technology transfer and advanced training in information technologies and telecommunications. INESC combines an entrepreneurial management with academic creativity which results in a special institutional flexibility. With regard to the organization of Scientific research and Technological Development Activities, these are presently structured in vertical scientific-technological areas, with strategic character and considered pertinent to the scientific and technological domains of activity are the following, by strategic area: Telecommunications and new services, Computers and informatics, Electronic systems and technology, Computer integrated manufacturing.

Large projects in these areas have been carried out internally and in their later phases have lead to products. An example that is worth mentioning is in the area of distributed and office systems. This led to two important products: the ELENIX office system and automation of the Portuguese PTT public postal services.

INESC has launched, in cooperation with IPE (Instituto de Participações do Estado), a business incubation center (AITEC). Several SMEs were created, some of them to bring the results of R&D projects of INESC into the market. In 1992, the Minister of Industry approved the creation by INESC of Technology Transfer Centers in the area of Tools for Open Systems and Information Systems, thus recognizing that INESC has good conditions as an institution to transfer its know-how in this areas to local industry.

8.2 Software AG

SOFTWARE AG, one of the top independent software suppliers worldwide, has long been a systems software supplier and has successfully added other areas in recent years. Its activities in the fields of consultancy, training and custom software development make SOFTWARE AG one of today's leading suppliers of comprehensive information processing services.

Established in 1969, SOFTWARE AG rapidly focused on international markets, particularly North America and Asia. Nowadays, around 80 per cent of sales are generated outside Germany, and SOFTWARE AG products are distributed by subsidiaries and partner firms in more than 60 countries worldwide. SOFTWARE AG is an international company, not bound by any inflexible, centralized management structures, but giving its national representatives the freedom to adapt to local market and social conditions.

SOFTWARE AG's position is strengthened by its financial independence, a factor which is underlined by the decision to change from a share holding structure into a trust. This transformation from a mere product supplier into a partner of its customers has already been completed at SOFTWARE AG and it can now look forward to future market success with new objectives and clearer strategies. Despite adverse economic conditions and worldwide recession, SOFTWARE AG was able to achieve a stable sales increase of 10% in 1992 (780 million DM). Positive domestic revenue made up for adverse conditions on the international foreign exchange market.

8.3 SMD Informatica

SMD Informatica is a Portuguese company created in 1987 as the result of R&D of INESC. The participation of INESC in the share capital of SMD, through AITEC-Tecnologias de Informação SA, guarantees a close connection with development and training in advanced technological areas.

SMD provides value added services that offer the appropriate solutions for large computer companies. The company also positions itself as an ISV, providing a large range of products for all the UNIX platforms. SMD is consolidating its internationalization, with the recent creation of SMD do Brasil Informatica (Brazil), as well as setting up business contacts with other countries (Spain, England, Switzerland, etc). The office automation solutions are based on a client/server architecture that provides a complete integration of our product line and offers a high degree of multi-vendor connectivity.

SMD has designed and developed a wide range of products from scratch, most of them with the cooperation of INESC. This set of products focuses on the office automation area (software and hardware).

8.4 NOVABASE

NOVABASE - Sistemas de Informação e Bases de Dados, S.A. is a joint-stock company created in May 1989 with the support of AITEC - Tecnologias de Informação, S.A.. NOVABASE is a technology based company that has a successful work done in the Portuguese market, specially in 4 key areas: health, education, justice, social security, agriculture and city councils. Most of NOVABASE's technicians worked as researchers at INESC, with combined expertise in the areas of information systems, databases, communications and artificial intelligence.

The technology and services provided by NOVABASE include: Development and Maintenance of Information Systems, Consulting and Training in Information Systems an Database Areas, Participation in R&D projects.

8.5 TASKON

Taskon AS is a company formed in 1988 for the purpose of supporting various categories of end users with individually tailored information systems by utilizing object-oriented technology. The company builds on technology developed during the past 15 years at the Center for Industrial Research and at Taskon with an investment of approximately 200 man-years. Taskon is a supplier of products for object-oriented system development and of total information systems integrating heterogeneous products from different vendors with Taskon's own solutions.

Taskon has over the past 5 years worked with object-oriented analysis and design of complex systems, and customization of information systems. In the period 1981-88 key personnel in Taskon worked at Center for Industrial Research with utilizing object-oriented technology in improving offshore engineering organizations and information systems. Taskon personnel has participated in several european cooperation projects: "PIMS" - Project Integrated Management System (ESPRIT 1 project), "REBOOT" - Reuse Based On Object oriented Techniques (ESPRIT 2 project), "PROTEUS" (ESPRIT 2 project), "ESF" - Eureka Software Factory (Eureka project).

8.6 EDP

EDP - Electricidade de Portugal, S.A. is one of the main Portuguese companies. EDP is devoted to the supplying, transmission and distribution of electrical energy, with a volume of sales (in 1992) around 2.5 million ECU, for a total of 4,5 million consumers. At present, EDP ensures about 95% of the total power demand of the Portuguese continent. To achieve its goals/purposes EDP has a complex structure based upon seven main Operational Divisions, covering all the functions typical of such an organization.

8.7 EDINFOR

EDINFOR - Sistemas Informaticos, S.A., is fully controlled (100%) by EDP. EDINFOR is a subsidiary company created in 1991, whose aim is to manage all the EDP database structures and to supply technical support and services. EDINFOR has currently a complete knowledge Facilities Management, overviewing the development of automatic integrated systems within the field of both services and industrial companies.

8.8 Comunicações Nacionais

Comunicações Nacionais (CN) was the top organization of a holding that includes the major telecommunication operators in Portugal (Telecom, TLP (Telefones de

Lisboa e Porto), Marconi, TDP). The role of Comunicações Nacionais is to coordinate the activities of the several companies of the holding. As the holding of the telecommunication companies in Portugal, the most desirable exploitation of results will be the dissemination of Orchestra technologies. If these prove successful, CN will provide a privileged channel to a very significant mass of users and customers.

8.9 UITESA

UITESA focuses its activities on technological consulting and advanced engineering services. For this it combines analysis of productive processes (such as physical phenomena simulation, reliability models and resources optimization, among others) and integration of operating support technologies (on line information systems, telecontrol, etc). The experience acquired by UITESA in the design, planning and operation of electrical power supply services, the multidisciplinary capacity it has developed, and its organizational flexibility to meet specific demands of customers are an assurance of the services it offers. The services of UITESA are mainly directed towards the utilities and Energy sectors and, in general, the industrial sector. UITESA is entirely owned by H.I. Holding (IBERDROLA Industrial Group) and is the leading company in the area of engineering.

IBERDROLA is an investor owned electric utility in Spain that generates, transmits and delivers electric power to almost 8 million customers located in a geographical area that covers more than 190,000 km2 with 16 million inhabitants. The total energy produced by its 16,700 Mw of installed capacity (50% hydro, 9% coal fired, 22% fuel-oil and gas, and 19% nuclear) amounts 45,000 Gwh. The 1992 revenue has been 8 billion ECU's.

8.10 ISCTE

ISCTE is the Faculty for Management Sciences of the Technical University of Lisbon. Its expertise includes Management, Sociology, Psychology and Applied Informatics. Besides educational activities, ISCTE provides general services in the areas of Management, Management Information Systems, Sociology and Social Anthropology.

8.11 LISLE

LISLE is an independent software company in Madrid, Spain. It provides services and software solutions in the Office Automation and Communications areas. It has close links with SMD S.A., participating in joint development, distribution and marketing activities.

8.12 UPM

The Universidad Politécnica de Madrid (UPM) has participated in the ORCHESTRA Project through the work developed by the Validation and Business Applications Group of the Artificial Intelligence Department. This Department as well as the Research Group whose experience in International as well as European Projects can be demonstrated permitted to assure a high level of professionalism and experience that were of vital importance to achieve the tasks entrusted to this entity.

This experience was especially valuable for the study and modelling of the problems of which this Research Group was in charge. One of these problems implied the original proposal of a model not existing up to now for a more efficient processing of the organizational problems and the development of the computing system supported by the ORCHESTRA Project.

The activities peculiar to a research group are among others the dissemination of the research results and the consequences of this dissemination are the diverse publications already issued or accepted for publication as well as others under preparation that will permit to make the international technical-scientific community know the works developed.

9. Dissemination of Results

9.1 Dissemination in the Industrial Forum

The Orchestra project has been publicized internally in the several institutions that take part in the Consortium. Examples of this dissemination has been the presentation of the Orchestra results in the 2nd Elenix User's Group Meeting, Lisbon, June 1996, by SMD, internal presentations at Software AG and in EDP (in the context of the PRIME programme).

9.2 Dissemination in the R&D

The teams that have disseminated the project's approaches and results in the Research community have been the INESC and UPM team, whose collaboration has proven fruitful. The dissemination takes the form of published paper or invited presentations or tutorials, which we list below.

- *"The E.U. Orchestra Project"* Conference presented by Jesús Cardeñosa at James Madison University, Virginia, USA, July 1994.

- *"The Automated Group Decision. The Orchestra Proposal"* Conference presented by Jesús Cardeñosa at George Washington University-Department of Management Science, USA, October 1994

- *"Beyond Formal Processes: Augmenting Workflow with Group Interaction Techniques"*. Pedro Antunes, Jesús Cardeñosa, Nuno Guimaraes, Javier

Segovia. Conference on Organizational Computing Systems (COOCS'95). Sheraton Silicon Valley, Milpitas, California, USA, August 13-16, 1995.

- *"Workflow Modeling, Automation and Augmentation : Enlightening Experiences in the ORCHESTRA project"*, N. Guimarães (IST/INESC), Ana Paula Pereira (INESC), NSF Workshop on Workflow and Process Automation in Information Systems, May 1996, Athens, GA, USA

- *"Managing Information in a Complex Organization"*. Jesús Cardeñosa, José Antonio Espinosa, Guillermo Pastor, Gilles Reyna. Interdisciplinary Workshop on Using Complex Information Systems (UCIS'96). Poitiers (France). September 4-6, 1996.

- *"Tecnologias de Informação na Transformação Organizacional - O projecto ORCHESTRA"*, Nuno Guimarães, Talk at the PRIMA Seminar - Process Industries Manufacturing Advantage, Electricidade de Portugal (EDP), November 16th 1996, Lisbon, Portugal

- *"Augmenting Work Environments: The Integration of Workflow Systems and Collaborative Work"*, Nuno M. Guimarães, invited for NATO Advanced Study Institute on Workflow Systems and Interoperability, Turkey, August 1997

10. Conclusion

This conclusion[41] is a set of comments concerning several aspects of the project that were not explicitly addressed in the previous chapters. Issues related with project management, schedules, and resources allocated and spent by the project are mentioned. A number of open directions, identified by the editor of this report and project manager, also deserve some reference.

10.1 Project Resources, Management, and Operation

The duration of the Orchestra project has been defined as two years. Looking back at the objectives and results that were achieved, this duration can be considered critical in several dimensions:

- From the point of view of the development of the technical components of Orchestra did not suffer from this limitation. Most of these components were in line with the interests, strategies and core businesses of the partners and no major shifts were observed, apart from those that were required for integration in a global environment like Orchestra. Moreover, it seems fair to say that a design and implementation that requires more than two years risks to be rapidly outdated when compared with the competition.
- The main problem with the schedule of the project had to do with the synchronization between the technical developments and their integration and test in the chosen pilots. The deployment of the Orchestra type of technology requires an initial phase of understanding of the project's objectives, a match

[41] These conclusions are, at the moment this first version of the final report is being released, more of a closing statement then an elaborated and prospective charter for the future of the Orchestra ideias and results. It is expected that the final discussions on the contents of this report bring additional contributions and enrich this "open" chapter of the document.

with the organizational needs, a significant amount of participatory design, and the allocation of resources for following up and experimenting the new developments. The experience of Orchestra shows that only in the later stages of the project could integration start to pay off, and therefore, a final period of experimentation and feedback could have been beneficial. The management of this relation between technical developments and the pilot sites has proven to be a very delicate area of the project, require more flexibility that it was anticipated. In fact, the mere processes of change that the companies of the pilot sites went through during the project (Comunicações Nacionais being closed, EDP being spliced into several companies) can have dramatic effects on approaches like the one followed by Orchestra.

The manpower resources were, when evaluated individually for each partner, fairly adequate. Shifts in the effort applied in the design and development occurred in particular areas due to options taken during the initial definition phases, which suggested the interest of new developments (e.g. the Fast Query system) or new design and architectures (e.g. the Workflow system). The main area were manpower fell short was (probably an endemic situation) in the integration area, along multiple dimensions. Examples of integration that required significant effort were: the link between the social sciences analysts (INDEG/ISCTE) and the providers of modeling tools (Taskon); the integration around the Orchestra/Elenix core which was undergoing development during the whole project, and was required to be stable in some areas; the integration (or support) of the pilots, specially the CONUC pilot, which was away from the operational location of SMD.

The Orchestra project has been managed by the project leader at INESC, a research and development institute which assumed the leadership of the project. The management resources were, apart from the coordinating partner, evenly distributed among the several partners. The experience showed that additional effort could have been beneficial. The coordination of the several teams took some time to refine and the setup of common integration and test platforms could have been carried out earlier in the project.

The tools and mechanisms used to manage and control the project were fairly standard and suggested by the conventional approaches of European projects: bimonthly reports, six month reports, cost statements; simple project management tools and (a lot of) electronic mail. General meetings have occurred regularly, although not with exceeding frequency: a kick off meeting in the first month of the project (1), preparatory general meetings before each six month review (3) , and the reviews themselves (3), in Lisbon (INESC), Lisbon (CN) and Madrid (CONUC), internal review meetings in the final stage (3) before the final review (1). The result was a total of eleven general meetings. The number of inter-partners interactions at the technical level is difficult to account for[42], but several aggregates could be identified: SMD, Novabase and INESC (User environment, workflow and security); SMD, Software AG and Edinfor (User environment, Global Information system); Software AG and Taskon (MEIS); INESC, Taskon and INDEG/ISCTE (Organizational Analysis and Modeling); INESC and UPM (Negotiation Tools).

10.2 Contributions and Open Directions

The consolidation of the project's ideas and approaches which, in spite of all wishes, did not occur until the project was already in execution, the design and developments of the several components, the experience in the integration, and the final thoughts and realizations that all the members of the project came across, allow us to identify a number of significant contributions in the technical domain. These contributions are evaluated here under a personal perspective, based on the experience gained in the project and on the observation of the external environment (existing products, research and development trends in the industrial and research arenas) and may or may not be transformed into competitive advantages of the several Orchestra products, depending on the subsequent efforts that each individual partner is willing to carry out.

10.2.1 Workflow Modeling

The approach adopted in Orchestra that separates the analysis and modeling of organizational aspects from their actual enactment by computer based tools, proved to be foresighted. In the area of workflow, the set of tools and methods that were designed and implemented anticipated a consolidated perspective that is emerging in communities like the one represented by the Workflow Management Coalition, which can be easily assumed to set the fundamental trends in the workflow area.

The definition of a separated Workflow engine, accessible and manipulated by external tools with the expressiveness and power of system analysis and design

[42] Following the Orchestra approach of mixing computer engineering and social sciences, a significant amount of electronic mail messages (around 1500 as seen from the project manager side), is available for analysis and production of sociograms (a technique for analyzing interpersonal relationships).

tools, like OORAM is a relevant contribution. The evaluation of existing tools and the feedback from research and development communities shows that the openness of workflow system architectures, together with the power of expression, analysis, reuse, and reasoning, of workflow programming tools are two of the most relevant attributes for product quality and competitiveness.

10.2.2 Legacy Systems Integration

The integration of corporate systems was evaluated in the scope of the Global Information system tasks in Orchestra. This integration effort was centered around the use of Software AG's technology and demonstrated the feasibility of relating personal and groupware computing with the areas traditionally left to the mainframe applications. In this domain, the results of Orchestra must be seen as proof of concepts and enlightening experiments that promote further integration. The most striking examples of this promising integration is a closer integration between workflow and corporate systems which, once again, will become a distinctive factor of future workflow systems.

10.2.3 Agent Mediated Communication

The Contextual Communication services designed and developed in Orchestra were, in its initial phases, an open area for innovation. The work performed in Orchestra demonstrated the usefulness and the technical feasibility of building organization-aware communication support components. This result falls clearly in the area of "agent supported communication", an area which, as analysis of market studies showed, is becoming of growing relevance (*"**Intelligent agent technology** - Intelligent agent technology (IAT) will be used to perform tasks on behalf of people. IAT has the ability to wait and watch for complex events and take action. Source: OVUM report of workflow technology*").

10.2.4 Augmentation of Work Processes

The success of workflow systems in particular areas of organizational work is undeniable. However, experience demonstrates that the level of automation provided by workflow systems, essentially based on the coordination of each individual's activities, does not consider a significant amount of work that occurs behind the scenes. The argument that workflow systems "automate a fiction" highlights the nature of real work as a mixture of formalized steps, and informal collaborative steps required for problem solving, decision and negotiation.

Orchestra has pioneered the proposal of methodologies and techniques to bridge the gap between the automation suggested by workflow systems and collaboration facilities provided by group meeting and decision tools. The approach initially exploited in Orchestra attempts to use group interaction support systems to solve exceptions and problems that occur in work processes. Problem identification tools, better integrated with workflow systems are a promising approach along this line.

A second approach, that has been suggested by the experience of Orchestra and in some sense closes the loop with the "Workflow Modeling" directions presented above, introduces the notion of group interaction at the workflow modeling stage. The consideration of group interaction at this level leads us to foresee modeling approaches look at how work "really occurs" instead of which "workflows" should be defined and should occur. This direction will therefore enable a choice between coordination- or collaboration- oriented solutions, which we believe to be more efficient and adaptive to the growing complexity of organizational structures and behaviors.

11. References

Appleton92
Appleton, E. L. "Smart Document Retrieval", Datamation, 20-23, January 15, 1992

Balenson 93
D. Balenson. *Privacy Enhancement for Internet Electronic Mail (Part III): Algorithms, Modes, and Identifiers*. RFC 1423, IAB IRTF PSRG, IETF PEM WG, February 1993.

Crocker 82
David H. Crocker (Reviewer). *Standard for the Format of ARPA INTERNET Text Messages*. RFC 822, University of Delaware, Newark, DE 19711, August 1982.

Daft84
Daft, R. , and Weick K. , Toward a model of organizations as interpretation systems.
Academy of Management Review, 9: 284 - 295., 1984

ENTIRE ACCESS manual, Software AG

ENTIRE NET-WORK manual, Software AG

ENTIRE BROKER manual, Software SG

Forsyth86
Forsyth, R. and Rada, R., "Machine Learning: Applications in Expert Systems and Information Retrieval", Ellis Horwood, 1986

Hammer93
M. Hammer and J. Champy, Reengineering the Corporation,
Nicholas Brealy Publishing, 1993

Jarrah92
Jarrah, A. I. Z., Bard, J. F. and de Silva, A. H., "A Heuristic for Machine Scheduling at General Mail Facilities", European Journal of Operational Research, 63, 192-206, 1992

Jing94
Jing, Y. and Croft, W. B., "An Association Thesaurus for Information Retrieval", University of Massachussetts at Amherst, MA, 1994

Kaliski 93
B. Kaliski. *Privacy Enhancement for Internet Electronic Mail (Part IV): Key Certification and Related Services.* RFC 1424, RSA Laboratories, February 1993.

Kent 93
S. Kent. *Privacy Enhancement for Internet Electronic Mail (Part II): Certificate-Based Key Management.* RFC 1422, IAB IRTF PSRG, IETF PEM, February 1993.

Kohl 93
J. Kohl and C. Neuman. *The Kerberos Network Authentication Service (V5).* RFC 1510, Digital Equipment Corporation and ISI, September 1993.

Lang94
Lang, K., "NewsWeeder: An Adaptative Information Filter", Thesis Proposal, Internal Document, School of Computer Science, Carnegie Mellon University, April 7, 1994

Lebowitz83
Lebowitz, M., "Intelligent Information Systems", Journal of the ACM, 1983

Linn 93
J. Linn. *Privacy Enhancement for Internet Electronic Mail (Part I): Message Encryption and Authentication Procedures.* RFC 1421, IAB IRTF PSRG, IETF PEM WG, February 1993.

McCusker, T. and Strauss, P., "Managing the Document Management Explosion", Datamation, 41-44, July 1, 1993

Marskah94
Workflow White Paper : An Overview of Workflow Software Proceedings of Workflow'94, San Jose, CA, 1994

Miles78
Miles, R. and Snow, C. , *Organizational strategy, structure, and processes.* New York: McGraw-Hill, 1978

Mintzber93
H. Mintzberg, Structure in Fives - Designing Effective Organizations, Prentice Hall, 1993

Mintzberg79
H. Mintzberg,Estrutura e Dinâmica das Organizações, Publicações D. Quixote, 1995, portuguese version of The Structure of Organizations, 1979, Prentice Hall

Morgan86
Morgan, G. , *Images of organizations.* Sage: Berverly Hills, 1986

Mukhopadhyay, U., Stephens, L. M., Huhns, M. N. and Bonell, R. D., "An Intelligent System for Document Retrieval in Distributed Office Environments", Journal of the ACM, 37 (3), 123-135, 1986

Neighbours, J. "Software Construction Using Components", Doctoral Dissertation, University of California, Irvine, California, 1981

Prieto Díaz, R. and Arango, G., "Domain Analysis and Software Systems Modelling", IEEE Computer Society Press, 1991

Porras87
Porras, J *Stream Analysis: a powerful way to diagnose and manage organizational change.*
Massachussets: Addison-Wesley, 1987

Quinn88
Quinn, R. *Beyond rational management: mastering the paradoxes and competing demands of high performance.* San Francisco: Jossey-Bass Publishers, 1988

Ross93
J.E. Ross,Total Quality Management, Kogan Page, 1993

Reenskaug95
Trygve Reenskaug, Working with Objects : the OORAM Software Engineering Method,
Manning Publications, 1995
Salton, G. and McGill, M., "Introduction to Modern Information Retrieval", McGraw Hill, New York, 1983

Sutcliffe, A. G. and Maiden, N. A. M., "A Theory of Domain Knowledge for Requirements Engineering", CITY University, 1994

SunRPC88
RPC: Remote Procedure Call Protocol Specification, Version 2. RFC 1057, Sun Microsystems, Inc., June 1988.

Stumpf 79
Judgment Decisions: A study of interactions among group membership, group functioning and the decision situation. S. Stumpf, R.Freedman, D. Zand. Academy of management Journal, 22, 765-782, 1979.

Vroom 88
The new leadership. Managing participation in organizations. V.Vroom, A.Jago. Ed. Prentice-Hall 1988.

Wray 93
J. Wray. *Generic Security Service API: C-bindings.* RFC 1509, Digital Equipment Corporation, September 1993.

Zegwaart 93
Erik Zegwaart. *Privacy Enhanced Mail in more detail.* Computer Networks and ISDN Systems, 25(Supl. 2):S63-S71, 1993.

Zimmermann 93
Philip Zimmermann. *Internal data structures used by pgp 2.3.* Manual Appendix, June 1993.

Appendix A
List of Actual (available) Documents & Prototypes

name of the document	authors
D 1.1.1 Report on the Diagnosis Methodology	Indeg/Iscte
D 1.1.2 Diagnosis of the Target Organisations	Indeg/Iscte
D 1.2.1 Evaluation on Target Organisations	Indeg/Iscte
D 1.3.1 Report on Taskon/OORam integration	Taskon
D 1.3.2 Description of Target Organizations	Taskon
D 2.1.1 Functional and Interface Description of Archive	SMD
D 2.1.2 Functional and Interface Description of Doc Generator	SMD
D 2.2.1 Functional and Interface Description of Workflow Tool	NOVABASE
D 2.3.1 Specification of the Security Architecture	INESC
D 2.4.1 Specification of Connectivity System and Interfaces	Software AG
D 2.4.2 Specification of Access and Manipulation	Software AG
D 3.1.1 Functional and Interface Description of Network	INESC
D 3.2.1 Specification of Formalisation and Classification	SoftwareAG/UPM
D 3.2.2 Specification of Distribution Tools	Software AG/UPM
D 4.1.1 Specification of MEIS	Software AG
D 4.1.2 MEIS Plug Specification	Software AG
D.4.1.3 Specification of Taskon/Integrator Integration	Taskon
D 4.2.1 Definition of Negotiation Architecture	UPM/INESC
P 4.2.1 Document - Prototype of Interactive Negotiation Tools	UPM/INESC
D 5.1.1 Platform and Systems Description	EDP
D 5.2.1 Platform and Systems Description	UITESA
D 5.3.1 Platform and Systems Description	CN
D 5.4.1 Platform and Systems Description	Taskon
D.6.1.1 Analysis of Competition	INESC
D 6.2.1 Market Analysis	INESC
D 6.3.2 Orchestra Product Definition	INESC

name of resulting prototype/installation	**available at/from**
P 2.1 - Archive system & Document Generator	SMD
P 2.2 - Workflow Tool	SMD
P 2.3 - Security system	INESC
P 2.4 - Connectivity & Data Access and Manipulation	Software AG
P 3.1 - Messaging Infrastructure	INESC
P 3.2 - Formalisation, Classification & Distribution	Software AG & UPM
P 4.1 - Integrated Taskon Integrator	Software AG & Taskon
P 4.2 - Interactive Negotiation Tools	INESC & UPM
P 5.1 - Pilot System I	EDP (outdated) & Edinfor
P 5.2 - Pilot System II	UITESA
P 5.3 - Pilot System III	*CN (no longer exists)*
P 5.4 - Pilot System IV	Taskon (BEST setup)

Your work in Orchestra had impact in other areas of your organization ?

	Yes (1)	No (0)
Total	21	2

Do you believe your results have a market potential ?

	Sim (1)	Não (0)
Total	21	2

Reasons for success or failure in the market (of your specific component)

	Success	Failure
INESC	• Process modeling is paramount in workflow integration • Extends the functionality of commercial products	
ISCTE	• Increasing integration between management and technology	
SMD	• Is very close to the market phase • Addresses needs like secure document management	
SAG	• Potentially useful applications for large companies • Market is open to this type of systems	
UPM	• Useful and easy to use • Reflects the organizational reality	• Too simple Database • Weak integration

Do you believe that the Orchestra results IN GENERAL, have a market potential ?

	Yes (1)	No (0)
Total	16	3

SMD Informatica				
José L. Mota, Mário Romão	SMD Informatica, Lg. Mov. Forças.Armadas,4, 2700 Amadora, Portugal	+351-1-4711004	+351-1-4711223	mar@smd.pt, jlm@smd.pt
Novabase				
José F. Sousa, Filipe Carlos	Novabase, Av.Ant.Jose Almeida,5F,6 1000 Lisboa, Portugal	+351-1-7959157	+351-1-7959188	jfs@novabase.pt, fnc@novabase.pt
Iscte/Semarte				
Luís A. Reto	Semarte, R.Américo Durão, Lt.14A,1°, 1900 Lisboa, Portugal	+351-1-8478179	+351-1-8478613	semarte@ mail.telepac.pt
Politecnica Madrid				
Jesus Cardeñosa	UPM - DIA, Campus Monteganceo, 28660 Boadilla del Monte, Spain	+34-1-3367436	+34-1-3524819	carde@fi.upm.es
TASKON				
Odd A. Lehne	Taskon A/S, Gaustadalleen 21, N-0371 Oslo, Norway	+47 22958617	+47 22604427	odda@taskon.no
LISLE				
Carlos Brazão	LISLE, Marte 210, 28760 Tres Cantos, Spain	+34-1-8037654	+34-1-8040207	euraitec@servicom.es

(updated May 1997)

Appendix C
Internal Survey - Questionnaires & Results

This appendix presents the results of an internal survey, coordinated by the INDEG/ISCTE team, that attemps to assess the opinions and evaluations made by the partners, through questionnaires presented to a set of individual persons belonging to the project teams. Some of the questions were presented to the more technically oriented teams, some others to the people in the pilot organizations, and some to both. From the number of answers, we observe that the sample can be considered significant (more than 20 answers in a universe of around 50 persons).

1. ORCHESTRA Results

How do you rate the interest of the Orchestra project ?

	Very High (5)	High (4)	Average (3)	Low (2)	Very Low (1)
Total	4	20			

How did you rate your understanding of the Orchestra project's objectives ?

	Very Good (5)	Good (4)	Enough (3)	Low (2)	Very Low (1)
Total	3	15	6		

How do you rate the understanding of the objective of your own technical task or objective ?

	Very Clear (5)	Clear (2)	Unclear (1)
Total	12	12	

Did you understand the specifications of your work in Orchestra ?

	Very Well (5)	Well (4)	Partially (3)	Hardly (2)	Very Hardly (1)
Total	11	12	1		

With which modules did your work have stronger relations ?

INESC	• Client-Server Communication • Archive, Elenix • Diagnosis & Modeling process • Workflow • Contextual communication
ISCTE	• Diagnosis • Modeling process • Workflow
Nova Base	• Workflow • Modeling system
SMD	• Workflow Elenix • Document generator • Server
SAG	• Contextual communication • Global information system • MEIS integration • Pilots
UPM	• Contextual communication • Distribution Rules • Contextual communication

How easy was the integration ?

	Vey Easy (5)	Easy (4)	Not Easy (3)	Hard (2)	Very Hard (1)
Total		8	6	7	2

Cause of the easiness or difficulties of the integration ?

	Things that made it easy	Things that made it hard
INESC	• Previous knowledge of the structure of the software where integration was performed	• Pilot data hard to transform directly into workflow information. • Lack of detailed technical doc on Elenix • Parallel evolution of the Elenix prototypes
ISCTE	• Dynamic Teams • Multidisciplinary competences of the several partners	• Weak involvement of the pilots • Pilots without an "organizational change" plan
Nova Base	• Possibility of joint work with SMD	

SMD	• Previous experience in client-server systems and architectures	• Some modules hard to integrate • Technical details • Weak cross-team communication
SAG		• Lack of a global and clear design of the system and of the interaction between the teams. • Heterogeneity of the tools and their unavailability at some pilots. • Schedule problems
UPM	• Well define interfaces in sone module	• Coordination problems • Insufficient information of the product specifications • Apriori choice of a software platform like Elenix

Do you expect "your" technical component to be used ?

	Yes (1)	No (0)	X
Total	22		

Which are the success factors of "your" technical component ?

INESC	• Better integration with other components • Integration of OORAM and Workflow Engine
ISCTE	• Colaboration of the pilots in the process of information gathering • Willingness in participating in "organizational change" processes • Appropriate contextualization in each organization
SMD	• Support of the client organization in the process of workflow implementation • Adaptation of the workflow to the organization and vice-versa • User Involvement
SAG	• Need for improvements and further experimentation • Productization of the Prototypes
UPM	• Integration in a groupware platform • Incoming documents withoot receiver specified • Better Integration with Elenix • Information Security and Database Management

Appendix B - Addresses and Contact Points

Name	Address	Phone	Fax	Email
INESC				
Nuno Guimarães, Pedro Antunes, Paula Pereira	INESC R.Alves Redol, 9, 6°, 1000 Lisboa , Portugal	+351-1-3100230	+351-1-3145843	nmg@inesc.pt, guimaraesn@acm.org, paa@inesc.pt, app@inesc.pt
Joao Gonçalves	(as above)	+351-1-3100524	+351-1-3145843	jmpg@eniac.inesc.pt
Armando Vieira	INESC, Av.Duque D'Avila 21, 1000 Lisboa, Portugal	+351-1-3100026	+351-1-3145843	amv@office1.inesc.pt
Software AG				
Jose A. Frias, Pedro Basagoiti, Fernando Garcia, Irma Trueba	Software AG Espana SA, Ronda de La Luna, 4, 28760 Tres Cantos, Madrid, Spain	+34-1-8079485	+34-1-8079447	jfrias@sag.es pbasagoiti@sag.es fgjulian@sag.es itrueba@sag.es
EDP				
João Amaral, Isabel Carapinha	EDP - Sines, S.Torpes, Sines, Portugal	+351-69-634421	+351-69-632680	
Leuschner Fernandes	EDP	+351-1-7263013	+351-1-7265870	
EDINFOR				
Carlos Raposo	EDINFOR, Av.Sidonio Pais,28,1D, 1000 Lisboa, Portugal	+351-1-3131300	+351-1-3561696	Carlos_Raposo_at_NOTES@calisto.edinfor.pt
UITESA				
Carmen Izquierdo	UITESA, Juan Bravo, 49D, 28006 Madrid, Spain	+34-1-3092036	+34-1-4014954	cic@uitesa.es
Telecom (ex-CN)				
Francisco Silva	Telecom, Gab.Rel.Int.-6.11, Av. Fontes Pereira Melo,40,6°, 1050 Lisboa, Portugal	+351-1-3504000	+351-1-579919	

Reasons for success or failure in the market (of ORCHESTRA results)

	Success	Failure
INESC	• The next step in office technology • First set of integrated technology • Interesting functionality	
ISCTE	• Support for multifaceted daily management of organizations	
SMD	• Need for participation of industrial partners	• Initial objectives were not reached
SAG	• Global product with global coverage • Requires clearer product decomposition	
UPM	• Covers many areas which are new to tradicional systems	• Not defined as a single product

2. Effort and Participation

What was the level of effort required by the participation in Orchestra ?

	very high (5)	high (4)	Fair (3)	Low (2)	Very Low (1)	X
Total	1	14	8	1		

What required greater effort ?

	Understand objectives	Design work	Carry out the tasks	Prepare meetings	Financial Mngt	Integrate Compnts
Total	2	9	14	1	2	1

3. Project Management

What is your oppinion of the project management concerning the amount of information provided to you and your organization ?

	Too much (5)	Enough (4)	Little (3)	Too little (2)	None (1)
Total		14	1	5	2

and concerning the control of the system installation and development at your organization ?

	Too much (5)	Enough (4)	Little (3)	Too Little (2)	None (1)
Total	1	8	6	1	

and concerning the support to integration with other partners' work ?

	Too much (5)	Enough (4)	Little (3)	Too Little (2)	None (1)
Total		8	10	5	

and concerning support to the financial and administrative management ?

	Too much (5)	Enough (4)	Little (3)	Too Litle (2)	None (1)
Total		11	4	3	

4. CONSORTIUM and this type of projects

How do you rate the number of partners in the Consortium ?

	Too large (3)	OK (2)	Too small (1)	X
Total	13	9		

If you could change the number and type of partners in the Consortium, what would you do ?

	Industrial Partners		Research Partners		Support partners		Pilots	
	More	Less	More	Less	More	Less	More	Less
Total	2	9	3	5		11	1	13

Duration of the Project?

	Too long (5)	Long (4)	OK (3)	Short (2)	Too short (1)
Total			13	8	

How do you rate the impact of this type of projects ?

	Personally		Organizationally		Participants	
	Pos	Neg	Pos	Neg	Pos	Neg
Total	17		16		13	

6. Final Conclusions

	Strong points	Weak Points
INESC	• Contact with industrial world • Development of a product with interesting potential • Enrichment of an office system	• Coordination between research and industrial objectives • Underestimation of the problems in sw enginnering • Too many partners • hard integration • Heterogeneous platforms • Schedule problems • Weak control in the pilots
ISCTE	• Partners' technical competence • Positive coordination of the project • Integrated vision with a new technology as the starting point	• Too many pilots • Pilots not open to change
SMD	• Competent Partners • Tecnological relevance • Interest to the market • Incresed know-how about other realities • Existence of pilots • Results close to industrialization • Production of a new generation groupware system	• Tendency to consider the project a second priority against the daily activities of the companines. • Weak communication among partners
SAG	• Experience interchange • Improvements in Know-How • Diversity of platforms • Market Amplitude	• Too much management • Hard collaboration • Too many partners • Unclear objectives
UPM	• Originality • Design	• Coordination • Validation Plan

Can you suggest some improvements ?

INESC	Smaller number of partners and pilots
ISCTE	Use pilots that want to get involved in a process of change
SMD	Structure the technical work into sub groups that have clearer objective and handle the integration efforts from the beginning
SAG	
UPM	Inprove coordination among partners

Questionnaires from the pilots

1. Installation and use of the Base Technology (Elenix Multimedia)

Was this technology installed at your site ?

	Yes	No
EDINFOR (EDP)	X	
UITESA	X	

When was the installation made ?

EDINFOR (EDP)	End 94 and March 96
UITESA	Set 94

Installations and users

	Installations	Users
EDINFOR (EDP)	5	5
UITESA	10	10

Which were the used functionalities (and the ones not used)

	Used	Not used
EDINFOR (EDP)	• Mail • Fax	
UITESA	• Mail • Fax • Agenda • Archive	• Search

What has been the frequency of use ?

	Daily	Weekly	Monthly
EDINFOR (EDP)			X
UITESA		X	

Which functionality would you like to have used (but did not) ?

	Functions	Why
EDINFOR (EDP)	Workflow	not available
UITESA	Search	Elenix not used as an archive and document management

3. RESULTS of the ORCHESTRA project

Are you aware of the results of the project ?

	Yes	No
EDINFOR (EDP)	X	
UITESA	X	

Which results do you consider more interesting ?

EDINFOR (EDP)	• Fast query prototype • Workpackage 2 results • Contextual communication • Decisional models
UITESA	• Contextual communication

Which results can be integrated in your organizations's infrastructure ?

EDINFOR (EDP)	• Fast query • Contextual communication

Are there formal plans in your organization for the introduction of systems like Orchestra ?

	Yes	No
EDINFOR (EDP)		X
UITESA		X

How was the experience in the project ?

	Positive	Negative
EDINFOR (EDP)	X	
UITESA		

Potential for market exploitation ?

EDINFOR (EDP)	• Some individual modules have opportunities
UITESA	• Yes

4. Effort and Participation

How was the effort to participate in the project ?

	Too large (5)	Large (4)	Fair (3)	Small (2)	Too small (1)	X
Total			9			

5. Project Management

What is your opinion in project management concerning the amount of information provided to you and your organization ?

	Too much (5)	Enough (4)	Little (3)	Too litlle (2)	None (1)	X
Total		5	4			

and concerning the control of the system installation and development at your organization?

	Too much (5)	Enough (4)	Little (3)	Too litle (2)	None (1)	X
Total			1	8		

and concerning the support to integration with other partners' work ?

	Too much (5)	Enough (4)	Little (3)	Too litle (2)	None (1)	X
Total		4	5			

6. Consortium and projects of this type

How do you rate the number of partners in the Consortium?

	Too large (3)	ok (2)	Too small (1)	X
Total	1	8		

If you could change the number and type of partners in the Consortium, what would you do ?

	Industrial Partners		Research Partners		Support partners		Pilots	
	More	Less	More	Less	More	Less	More	Less
Edinfor				1				1

(Edp)								
UITESA		8			8			8
Total		8		1	8			9

Duration of the Project ?

	Too long (5)	Long (4)	OK (3)	Short (2)	Too short (1)
Total	4		1	4	

7. FINAL Conclusions

What is the relevance of the involvement of top management in this kind of projects ?

EDINFOR (EDP)	• Motivation • Decision swiftness • Support project's activities and promote involvement of other levels in the company

Can you suggest some improvements ?

EDINFOR (EDP)	
CN	
UITESA	• Better product integration • Better partner coordination • Better followup of the pilots

Research Reports Esprit

Area *Peripheral Systems, Business Systems and House Automation*

Learning in Man-Computer Interaction. A Review of the Literature.
T. Bösser. XI, 218 pages. 1987 (Project 385 HUFIT, Human Factor Laboratories in Information Technologies, Vol. 1)

Automatic Tools for Designing Office Information Systems. The TODOS Approach. Edited by B. Pernici, C. Rolland. IX, 321 pages. 1990 (Project 813 TODOS, Vol.1)

Integrated Management of Technical Documentation. The System SPRITE. Edited by J. Hoppe. VIII, 244 pages. 1992 (Project 2001 SPRITE, Storage, Processing and Retrieval of Information in a Technical Environment, Vol. 1)

Integration of Graphics and OSI Standards. Edited by R.A. Day, D.A. Duce, J.R. Gallop, D.C. Sutcliffe. X, 157 pages. 1993 (Project 2463 ARGOSI, Applications-Related Graphics and OSI Standards Integration, Vol. 1)

The COMANDOS Distributed Application Platform. Edited by V. Cahill, R. Balter, N.R. Harris, X. Rousset de Pina. XVII, 312 pages. 1993 (Project 2071 COMANDOS, Construction and Management of Distributed Open Systems, Vol. 1)

Ultra-wideband Coherent Optical LANs. Edited by S. Forcesi. X, 97 pages. 1993 (Project 2054 UCOL, Vol. 1)

Cooperation Among Organizations. The Potential of Computer Supported Cooperative Work. Edited by R.J.D. Power. VII, 140 pages, 1993 (Project 5660 PECOS, Perspectives on Cooperative Systems, Vol. 1)

The OSI95 Transport Service with Multimedia Support. Edited by A. Danthine. VIII, 515 pages. 1994 (Project 5341 OSI95, High Performance OSI Protocols with Multimedia Support on HSLANs and B-ISDN, Vol. 1)

The Translator's Workbench. Tools and Terminology for Translation and Text Processing. Edited by M. Kugler, K. Ahmad, G. Thurmair. IX, 183 pages. 1995 (Project 2315 TWB, Vol. 1)

Advances in Human-Computer Interaction. Human Comfort and Security. Edited by S. Pfleger, J. Gonçalves, K. Varghese. XI, 323 pages. 1995 (Project Group HCI, Vol. 1)

Human Comfort and Security of Information Systems. Advanced Interfaces for the Information Society. Human Comfort and Security. Edited by K. Varghese, S. Pfleger. XIII, 320 pages. 1997 (Project Group HCI, Vol. 2)

Organizational Change, Evolution, Structuring and Awareness. Organizational Computing Systems. Edited by N. Guimarães. XI, 174 pages. 1998 (Project 8749 ORCHESTRA, Vol. 1)

Springer and the environment

MIX
Papier aus verantwortungsvollen Quellen
Paper from responsible sources
FSC® C105338

If you have any concerns about our products,
you can contact us on
ProductSafety@springernature.com

In case Publisher is established outside the EU,
the EU authorized representative is:
Springer Nature Customer Service Center GmbH
Europaplatz 3, 69115 Heidelberg, Germany

Printed by Libri Plureos GmbH
in Hamburg, Germany